BRIT-THINK AMERI-THINK

A Transatlantic Survival Guide

In writing this book, I've tried hard to be
even-handed, and fair to both sides. If there's
someone I haven't insulted .... I'm sorry.

BRIT-THINK
AMERI-THINK

A Transatlantic Survival Guide

Jane Walmsley

with cartoons by
Gray Jolliffe

HARRAP
LONDON

To my daughter Katie ...
who has an American mother
and a British father, and
is — as she puts it — 'haff and hawf'.

First published in Great Britain 1986
by HARRAP LTD
19-23 Ludgate Hill, London EC4M 7PD

Text © Jane Walmsley 1986
Cartoons © Gray Jolliffe 1986

ISBN 0 245-54337-6

Designed by Robert Wheeler

Printed and bound in Great Britain
by Redwood Burn, Trowbridge

Contents

1 First things first

The *Language* of Anglo-Ameri-think

Confused? You won't be. Just remember that:

UK		US
chips	=	french fries
crisps	=	potato chips
biscuit	=	cookie or cracker
scone	=	biscuit (baking powder)
crumpet	=	UNKNOWN
UNKNOWN	=	English muffin
tart	=	hooker
ground floor	=	first floor
first floor	=	second floor
vest	=	undershirt
waistcoat	=	vest
knickers	=	underpants
knickerbockers	=	knickers
lorry	=	truck
van	=	pickup
juggernaut	=	big (mother) truck
pickup	=	hooker
fag	=	cigarette
poof	=	fag
wally	=	jerk
jerk	=	off

... and so on. But, translating words and phrases is the easy part. It takes years of Anglo-Amerexperience to understand *the thinking behind them* ... and that's the hard part.

George Bernard Shaw said it best, though many have said it badly ever since. America and Britain are two nations divided by a common language. Between us is a Great Philosophical and Cultural Divide,

A TYPICAL MISUNDERSTANDING

which is obscured by the familiar lingo. Our respective heads of government may burble on about 'common bonds' and 'special relationships' — but the truth is that, in the 80s, Brit-think and Ameri-think are light years apart. We cherish widely different values and aspirations, and have developed separate habits of mind. Only the names remain the same ... and there's some doubt about those (see above). In some ways, a camel and a porpoise have more in common.

That's the bad news. But, dedicated travellers and internationalists take heart. The *good* news is that — with no language barrier to overcome — you've a once-in-a-lifetime opportunity to penetrate a foreign mind. So, if you've been perplexed by the trans-Atlantic psycho-gap, and feel that your holidays (or business dealings) will be enhanced if only you can bridge it — then here's a guide to basic Brit-think and Ameri-think. Mind-reading for the jet-set.

8

Basic Brit-think and Ameri-think:
The most important things to know

1 I'm gonna live for ever

AMERI-THINK: The single most important thing to know about Americans — the attitude which *truly* distinguishes them from the British, and explains much superficially odd behaviour — is that *Americans think that death is optional.* They may not admit it, and will probably laugh if it's suggested; but it's a state of mind — a kind of national leitmotiv if you like — that colours everything they do. There's a nagging suspicion that you can delay death (or, who knows, avoid it altogether) if you really try. This explains the common pre-occupation with health, aerobics, prune-juice, plastic surgery and education.

The idea is that you're given one life to live, and it's up to you to get it right. You should:

● use the time to maximize individual potential (have a nose-job, get a college degree) so as to ensure the highest-quality life possible.

● take care of your body so it will last. If extended life-span — or even immortality — proves possible, at least you're ready.

That's the secret of America's fundamental optimism; but it's not as cheery as it sounds. It imposes on the individual a whole range of duties

and responsibilities. Your life is in your own hands ... and the quality of that life as well. You owe it to yourself to be beautiful, clever, skinny, successful, and healthy. If you fail, it's because you're not trying hard enough ... (you didn't jog regularly, you should've eaten more bran). Death becomes your fault.

BRIT-THINK: Brit-think on the subject is fundamentally different, and accounts for the yawning gulf in national attitudes. Brits keep a weather eye on the Sword of Damocles, suspended above their heads. Lives are to be lived with a certain detachment, and a sense of distance preserved. One rolls with the punches. It's fruitless to try and take control, bad form to get too involved, arrogant and self-important to attempt to outwit destiny.

Events must be allowed to run their natural course. Stay cool, and *never* be seen to try too hard (Americans are so intense!) since anyone with half-a-brain should recognize the central absurdity of existence (Monty Python was so apt) and accept the inevitable. Success — if it's to count — must appear effortless. Since nothing matters very much anyway, think twice before making important sacrifices. Never run for a bus. Never skip tea.

2 New is good

AMERI-THINK: Meet an American for the first time, and he's likely to greet you with, 'so, what's new?' (abridged in Manhattan to 'so, new?') He wants more than a general progress report. One small part of him means it literally, begging an answer like, 'well, I've got a new Chevy/lover/food processor'. Because in America, *new* is *good*. Americans are the world's greatest believers in progress. Life gets better all the time — or should. They expect a 70-year crescendo, starting at not-so-hot, and rising to terrific.

Nothing will convince a True American (even an elderly one) that 'things were better "way back when"'. They point in evidence at the history of modern medicine: once there was smallpox, now there isn't. Old things can be treated with a certain irreverence, since something better is always just around the corner. *America* is still new — still warm and gently throbbing — and so are the most desirable things in it. Over much of the country new property attracts a higher price than old, new shopping malls snatch customers from 'old' haunts as soon as they cut the ribbon on the parking lot. New products are greeted with enthusiasm, since advanced versions always include 'improvements'.

10

No point in clinging grimly to the past, or we'd never have traded gramophones for colour TV's, buckshot for Star Wars, or headaches for coated aspirin.

BRIT-THINK: Life — and the simple passage of time — does *not* pre-suppose progress. At best, there are large flat areas. There's little proof that things get better, and a great deal of evidence to suggest the opposite. Look at defence: we live with the threat of the Big Bang. Look at architecture: Victorians built better houses than we do. Look at world affairs: we have to waste time listening to the ravings of Muslim lunatics. Look at sportsmanship: it was fairer play before they invented steroids. Look at AIDS. That's new.

True Brits loathe newness, and display a profound fear of change. They see modern life as increasingly uncertain, events as random, and 'untried' ideas as undesirable. Even small changes can cause Britt-trauma, with the nation shaken to its roots at suggestions that traditional red 'phone boxes may be painted yellow. Far better to preserve the status quo, to hope that custom and ritual will somehow counter the capriciousness of fate. (Britain is the heartland of 'We've Always Done It This Way'.) Conclusion: change nothing unless forced. Remember that God usually gets it right first time.

3 Never forget you've got a choice

AMERI-THINK: Choice — lots of it — is as dear to the American heart as newness. The point about choice is to exercise it as much as possible. That's why Yanks *elect* so many people: Presidents, governors, judges, senators, congressmen and dog-catchers.

Americans never commit themselves to anything for life. Leaders you can't change — like Monarchs — make them nervous. They reserve the right to review decisions periodically; anything less is an attack on personal freedom, and reminds them of Communism. They even get edgy when fruit they like is out of season. Limited choice makes them think of Moscow matrons queuing hopelessly for goods. Nowhere do people view restrictions with more alarm. They mistrust package holidays and long-term investments. Contracts of employment must contain appropriate 'get out' clauses. They plan vacations and shop for Christmas at the last minute, and make final decisions only when they've considered all possible choices. They conduct business by 'phone, and avoid committing anything to paper. They don't even like

11

restaurants with set menus. The right to substitute a tossed salad for french fries is enshrined in the Constitution. Americans like to live life à la carte.

BRIT-THINK: The range of personal choice must be strictly limited. (This is reflected in the retail industry, where dresses come in four sizes, shoes in one width, and ice cream in three flavours.) Too many options only confuse people, and encourage them to behave in a greedy and selfish way. It's part of human nature to be happier when our horizons are limited, someone else is in charge, and we know what's expected of us. That's why Monarchs are so useful, and the class system survives. It's also why we enjoyed such widespread national contentment during the Second World War. All you had to know was how many coupons were left in your ration book. All appearances to the contrary, the heat was off.

Since then, the argument goes, it's been downhill all the way. More options and higher expectations have spawned the 'Me' generation, which doesn't understand the relationship between virtue and restriction. It'll end in tears or *anarchy* (which is British for 'unlimited choice').

4 Smart money

AMERI-THINK: Choice (see opp.) is the same thing as freedom, which is the same thing as money, and that's the real secret of the national fondness for cash. It's not that Americans are by nature greedier or more acquisitive than their European counterparts. They're no fonder of their dishwashers and micro-waves than the British of their colour TV's and double glazing ... no happier with their automatic orange-juicers and garbage compactors in Houston than a Liverpool housewife with a toasted sandwich-maker or a duvet. Nor do Pennsylvania steelworkers push harder for wage-settlements than Yorkshire miners. It's just that Americans admire money more openly. They see it as a measure of success, and the final guarantee of personal choice. In short, Money is Power — and power is a good thing. Lack of power makes you a Shlep. Money is a hedge against Shlep-hood.

Furthermore, you *can* take it with you — or, if you've got enough, you may not have to go. Cash gives room for manoeuvre. If it turns out that death *is* optional — or science comes up with a commercial miracle — your dollars guarantee that you won't be ignored. Money buys the best ... and the best is your birthright.

BRIT-THINK: Public stance of middle-to-upper classes is to poo-poo money ('not my first priority') and instead to speak passionately of 'the quality of life'. By this, Brits mean things spiritual or cultural, which — they maintain — have nothing to do with hard cash. Price of theatre tickets notwithstanding.

The theory is that money can't buy taste, or style, or a sense of priorities — which are things you're born with. (Wealthy people are born with more than poor ones.) Your spending habits are seen as a reflection of breeding and the quality of your mind, and allow others to make judgements about your background and personal style. Haggling about money is OK for miners and steelworkers (just). Others should concern themselves with loyalty to employers, or duty to the wider community. It is the custom of wealthiest Brits (Captains of Industry and/or Royals) to periodically remind the masses of the virtues of self-denial and restraint. This is called *noblesse oblige*.

Single-minded pursuit of The Readies is simply vulgar, and undermines the human spirit. Of course, you've got to *have* money —because penury is unbecoming, and gets in the way. But enough is enough. After all — you can't take it with you. Americans never understand that.

5 The consensus society

AMERI-THINK: Yup, that's what they call it. What they mean is that virtually everyone in America — be he farmer, welder or Wall Street wizard — wants the same thing. Their separate definitions of 'the good life', if you asked them, would be amazingly similar. Nor do any of them — regardless of financial position — tend to question the fundamental social order. With the exception of a few ageing refugees from Haight-Ashbury, America in the Eighties is sure it's got it right. The nation's politics reflect this. There's not much ideological distance between the two major parties. Sure, the Republicans are supposed to favour Big Business, lower taxes and centralized government, while Democrats are traditionally more liberal, freer public spenders, and happier to devolve decisions. But they're all after the same *result* — a strong, secure and unabashedly capitalist America.

BRIT-THINK: ***'Them 'n Us'***

Politics in Britain is a Civil War without weapons. Even elections do not buy us a period of peace and quiet — the losers will not accept the result.

Brian Walden
The *London Standard*

14

Of course they won't, when whole sections of the community see their personal interests as irrevocably bound up in the fortunes of one particular party. It's a war all right, between the 'them' side and the 'us' side, and it's a fight to the death. No chance of defeat with honour; no reconciliation, no magnanimity. Winner takes all, and the loser retires to sulk in a corner for four or five years.

You don't *choose* your side of the Body Politic; you're born there. To break away represents a betrayal of class and family. Your Party is You, and vice-versa. It is on your side, even when it is wrecking your prospects and the economy of the nation. To Brits, party loyalty has nothing to do with pragmatism, and abject failure is no good reason for desertion. No: Brit-politics are not really about personal *gain*. They are about class dominance and principles. Compromise with the Other Side is dangerous, since it blunts the cutting edge of despair. Co-operation . . . what's that? This is why Brits conclude that all forms of progress are impossible. They are right. Under the present system, nothing moves.

6   'Me-think' vs. 'We-think'

AMERI-THINK: *'Moi — I come first' (the Piggy Principle)*

Miss Piggy said it, and touched a chord deep in the hearts of her countrymen. An American considers that his first duty and obligation is to look after Number One. This follows on from 'I'm gonna live forever', because it stands to reason that you've got to take care of yourself if you're going to last. If each person concentrates on attaining his 'personal best' — and achieves inner fulfilment — we will have created a better society.

Without knowing it, most Yanks support the ideas of Adam Smith — the economist who advanced the theory that the individual working in his own interests leads ultimately to the greatest good of the State. A strong society is merely the sum of strong parts. It's often said that America is the heartland of individualism . . . and this is what people mean. You protect your own interests by making choices — lots of them. If you've acquired money — which gives you more leverage — then so much the better. It is no accident that Frank Sinatra scored a monster hit with 'I Did It My Way'. Frankie understands 'Me-think'.

'Piggy-think' does not sit easily with Brits. It strikes them as selfish, and a bit brutal. Whether they vote Tory or Labour, they've spent years living under various permutations of Socialist government. This has created different habits of mind, and softened the collective rhetoric. 'Moi — I come first' — sticks in the throat. Brits of most persuasions are happiest talking about 'self-reliance' and 'the common good', which reminds them of The War, the Crown and the BBC in no particular order. This has a great deal of social credibility, but — paradoxically — often turns out to mean 'my right to do what's best for me, and hope that your requirements don't get in the way'.

Culturally, socially, psychologically, *literally* — Brits form orderly queues. They like to keep things nice and cosy. Fundamental to 'we-think' is the dread of inciting a contest — a scrum. Brits are by nature reluctant to throw down the gauntlet; and 'I come first' is a challenge to others — notification of battle. Strong stuff, where there are winners and losers, and the weak go to the wall. Once the gloves are off, no one can predict the outcome.

This carries with it the risk of change, blood-letting, and general social turbulence. (No Shake-ups, Please — We're British.) 'We-think' creates the impression of a kinder, more caring society, where rich and poor alike are cushioned against the harsh realities of unbridled competition. One can't win by much, or lose by much. So goes the Brit-myth.

7   Good Guys and Bad Guys

BRIT-THINK: *Selfish* people (those who raise a finger or two to 'we-think') can always get the jump on others. These include:

1   Those who have made lots of money in property or trade (but not those who have inherited it). To take an *active* role — to strive — is to invite censure. *Passive* good fortune gets you off the hook, since it's not your fault you're loaded.

2   Manual workers on strike for more pay, who turn out — infuriatingly — to have real bargaining leverage. This is called 'holding the public to ransom'. The popular Brit-press then assumes the role of 'the striker's conscience'. Power-workers are exhorted to 'consider the elderly' before turning off the juice. Railway workers are cautioned that action will 'only hurt the

commuter' ... or nurses and teachers that 'patients and children will suffer'. It is hoped that this will remind them of 'we-think', and make them ashamed to exploit an obvious industrial advantage.

Ordinary Brit-citizens are automatically expected to place 'vocation' or a sense of 'duty to the wider community' before personal concerns like the right amount of hard cash. This applies to nurses, power, water and railway workers, miners and teachers ... but not to doctors, Cabinet Ministers, top Civil Servants, or Captains of Industry. Logic also inverts in the case of the Queen, who is perceived as the embodiment of 'we-think' — a woman who regards duty as the highest privilege — despite a personal fortune worth billions of pounds. According to classic Brit-think, she is seen as self-sacrificing, socially virtuous, *and* rich.

AMERI-THINK: More 'me-think'. No expectation of high social ideals from Joe Average. No concept of 'Pleb-Oblige'. Make no mistake: Americans are charmed by altruism when they find it; but it is not regarded as compulsory for the lower social orders.

Yanks are the world's biggest sceptics when it comes to human motivation, since they take it for granted that — with the exceptions of Mother Teresa and Bob Geldof — others are busy looking after Number One. There are only two certainties in life, and both should be borne firmly in mind:

1 everybody likes ice cream
2 every man/woman has his/her price

Undiluted 'me-think' irritates Brits, who fear:

1 that Yanks perceive only the basest motives, and
2 that they're probably right.

One last cultural point: Yanks loathe *sharing*, which is incompatible with 'me-think'. They specially hate the British practice of sharing restaurant tables with complete strangers. No American hotels — even the oldest ones — were built with shared bathrooms. Shops have no communal fitting-rooms. Only dire financial constraint will induce anyone to accept a party telephone line. There is only *one* thing a Yank will share with any equanimity. His dessert.

2 Brits and Yanks abroad . . . business and pleasure (. . . as others see us)

AMERI-STYLE: Generally speaking, Yanks abroad come in two varieties: groomed and casual. Age has little to do with categories, since you can fit into either at 16 or 70. Geriatrics in stretch denims are not uncommon. Neither are 6-year-olds in fur coats.

Commonly, the American travelling abroad for pleasure is casual, but *equipped.* He's got the most expensive 'walking shoes' money can buy, and these are hideously ugly but orthopedically correct. His wardrobe is largely composed of crush-proof petroleum by-products. He has nylon-coated rainwear and fold-away hats, collapsible umbrellas and light-weight high-resolution sound videocam. There's a pocket calculator to work out his restaurant tips, convert pounds into piastres or kilograms, wake him in the morning and deliver regular updates on the New York Stock Exchange. He has brought with him a battery-powered tooth-brush, an electrical converter and matching water-pic. He's got a separate case for double quantities of all vital medications and a spare pair of soft lenses, plus a container of dental floss in case the water-pic breaks down.

Amer-Executive

When travelling abroad, he is groomed to corporate perfection. He is careful to look prosperous, heterosexual and clean. His fingernails are immaculate as a dentist's, and beautifully buffed. He appears to believe that many an important business deal rides on the quality of his manicure.

He wears the statutory Burberry raincoat-with-plaid-lining over his 400-dollar suit, which may have a matching waistcoat, but is in any case a nice mid-gray pin-stripe or herring-bone from Brooks or Saks. It hits perfectly on the shoulders.

His hair is as neat as his nails. If it's thick enough, he wears it cut like JFK's; if there's grey at the temples, he leans toward Blake Carrington. He hopes to look like a Kennedy-clone, or at least a graduate of Harvard Business School. In fact, he's been to Syracuse or U. Ohio . . . or (if over 45) nowhere.

Wrist-watches are important. He prefers tasteful traditional with lizard strap, or Cartier tank (the gen. article). Above all, no lumpy chronometers. His briefcase is fine calfskin, unscathed by the journey through three different airports (when travelling, he slips it inside a protective drawstring cover).

He is the living incarnation of that popular East Coast adage, 'dress British, think Yiddish'. He knows that Yanks are perceived abroad as garish and tasteless dressers, and wants to avert the charge. There's not a thread of Madras plaid, or polyester or ultra-suede in his Louis Vuitton luggage. He's purchased with care, to appear understated but unmistakably prominent. He doesn't understand that *British* for understated but unmistakably prominent is SCRUFFY (as in Chancellor of the Exchequer's briefcase).

Ameri-wife

Her role-models are drawn from *Dallas* and *Dynasty*. She sees herself as the 'new woman', peddled constantly on the covers of *Vogue* and *Good Housekeeping*. She knows you can BE FABULOUS AT 40, TURN HEADS AT 50. Look at Raquel and Jane. Look at Joan and Sophia. Look at Sue Ellen.

For the past two weeks, Ameri-wife has doubled up on her California stretch classes and tennis lessons back home in Houston, in preparation for her trip. She shed a few pounds for Europe, so as to indulge in pasta and croissants with a free mind. But, each time she eats, her waistbands get tighter, and — unable to convert stones to pounds — she longs for the reassurance of her digital bathroom scale. Already, she's liberated the laxatives from her husband's 'medications' suitcase, and is pre-occupied with regularity (Europeans should eat more roughage).

Wardrobe includes pastel-coloured parachute suits and matching Nike sports shoes for sightseeing, with plenty of chunky gold jewellery. (Loves 'anything deco'.) Hair is the blonde-streaked mane of a Texas lioness, a bit long for her age, but 'look at Dyan Cannon'. Anyway, 'he won't let me cut it!'

Ameri-wife enthuses a great deal about visiting ancient sites, museums and theatres, but what she's really looking forward to in London is a chance to *shop*. She'll buy more place-settings of her favourite Staffordshire dinner service, and some Waterford crystal 'so much cheaper than in Houston'. She'll stock up on cashmeres, Boots mascara and anything Burberry. Then, if there's time left, she'll spend it looking for 'cute places to have lunch'. (See 'Cute', Chapter 9.)

There follows a list of *Cute Places To Have Lunch* within easy radius of *Cute Places to Shop* in London.

Bond Street/South Molton Street area

Coconut Grove Restaurant, St Christopher's Place
Widow Applebaum's Delicatessen, South Molton Street
South Molton Street Creperie
Fenwick's Cafeteria, 2nd Floor, Fenwick's Department Store, Bond Street
The Place to Eat, 3rd Floor, John Lewis, Oxford Street
The Chicago Pizza Pie Factory, 17 Hanover Square (Great stuffed mushrooms!)

Knightsbridge
Harvey's At The Top (Harvey Nichols Department Store)
Harvey's downstairs Cafeteria (Harvey Nichols basement)
Harrods Dress Circle (Harrods 1st floor)
Harrods Westside Cafe (Harrods Ground Floor)
Joseph Pour La Maison (downstairs café inside Joseph's shop of the same name, Sloane Street)
Fantasie Brasserie (Knightsbridge Green)
San Lorenzo (Beauchamps Place)
Menage A Trois (fav. Royal watering hole, Beauchamps Place)
Brasserie St Quentin (Brompton Road, Knightsbridge)
Mr Chow's (Chinese lunches), Knightsbridge

Burlington Arcade/Green Park
The Ritz Hotel (book ahead for teas), Piccadilly
Cecconi's (dressy Italian)
Langan's Brasserie (Stratton Street, Mayfair)
Fortnum's Fountain (Fortnum and Mason Department Store, ice cream to the gentry)

Covent Garden
Joe Allen Restaurant (underground at 13 Exeter Street)
Le Café Des Amis du Vin, Hanover Place
Smiths, Shelton Street
Creperie in the Garden
Orso's, Wellington Street

Brits on US hols ... *a word of warning*

Some Euro-visitors dislike 'commercial' hotels — i.e., anything with a 24-hour coffee shop, hi-speed elevators and working plumbing. America has no other kind. Brits will waste a great deal of time and face certain disappointment if they persist in searching for 'something with character' — i.e., akin to British hotels which offer temperamental plumbing and *no* services, but charge you even more.

A Brit goes Stateside

He is somehow the antithesis of the Somerset Maugham figure: the man kitted out in a tropical cream-coloured suit with matching Fedora, languorously sipping mint tea under whirling ceiling fans and avoiding mad dogs and the noonday sun. It seems that, when the Empire struck back, the Brit-sense of tropical attire took a direct hit.

America in summer can be a hot place, and the visiting Brit often exudes — discomfort. He looks a bit frayed at the edges, and generally is as *under*-equipped as his American counterpart is *over*. This has nothing to do with income-group. It is a policy decision. So, he does not have the converter and the water-pic. He does not even have much of a toothbrush. He's purchased no extra clothes for the journey, and the ones he has make no concession to the climate ... 'no point, when I'll only be there for a week or two'. He is 'making do' by wearing the trousers to an old office suit, teamed with a short-sleeved Aertex shirt. It has a cream background (he dislikes the 'glare' of pure white) and has a way of looking soiled in strong sunlight.

Feet are clad in dark City slip-ons, because the only casual shoes he owns are wellies ('for the gardening'), some old cricket shoes and bedroom slippers. If caught short, he'll splash out on a pair of rubber foam flip-flops half-way through the holiday, but only after he's been forced to wear his City slip-ons down to the beach.

The sun presents real problems; he burns if he stands for too long under a strong light-bulb. So he wears lots of protective cream (his one item of special expenditure) and always needs help in applying it to his back. He discovers that his bathing trunks are revealing by American standards (Yanks consider anything skimpier than boxer shorts as *de facto* flashing). He has *not* bought a matching cover-up (*de rigueur* by US pools) and appears every day sporting yesterday's Aertex, unbuttoned to the waist to reveal gradually reddening chest. He has *not* invested in swish sunglasses ('£30 for *those*?') and instead has shades that clip on over his prescription glasses. For some reason, he usually wears them flipped *up*.

Mrs Brit

So does his wife. If she is middle-aged, she is his counterpart — but slightly better equipped. For instance, she has sandals. They're robust, tannish leather flatties with lots of buckles to adjust the width, and owe more to Dr Scholl than to high fashion. But they are comfy, especially as her ankles tend to swell and she 'retains water in hot climates' (anything with temperatures higher than Reykjavik). She never quite gets to grips with tropical sun-colours ('too garish, like Hawaiian shirts') and instead favours subdued shades of sage green-to-grey ... 'more tasteful and flattering'. Cream is nice, especially with sage green, avocado or brown (or all together). At heart, she is happiest wearing the colours she's used in the lounge.

She worries excessively about *food* ... not about gaining weight, or cholesterol or regularity, but about getting 'gyppy tummy' (the runs). She worries even in 'sanitary' countries like the US, and has strange theories about what causes it ('raw onion with hamburger, too much ice in drinks, air-conditioning everywhere, even in cars'). She doesn't care for the tea, the coffee, the cooking or the salad dressing, is 'if-y' about the bread ('what's a bagel?') but approves of the variety of fresh produce ('quality is nice ... such a good seasonal selection!'). Worries that the consumption of too much soft fruit will end in tears — or other moisture in the wrong places. Gyppy tummy.

Brit grooverette

The younger woman has her act together, sartorially at least. She's bought playsuits in pastel crushed cottons, and sexy off-the-shoulder T-shirts for the discos (except that, at American resorts she can't find

23

many, so repairs often to the local hamburger-and-singles-bar). Her accent is a Godsend, and for the first time in her life she's told it's 'gorgeous' — even if she comes from Liverpool or Birmingham. She finds that a grooverette's reputation for sexual rapacity precedes her (somehow borne out by her pink-tipped, wet-gelled hair, and selection of earings hanging from one multiply-pierced lobe).

In truth, she's something of an innocent abroad, never having been far out of mum's earshot. But she enjoys her notoriety, and laughs a lot, and likes being teased even when she doesn't understand the jokes. People always say she's 'so cute' when she says 'chips' instead of french fries. (See 'Cute', p. 67.) She doesn't mind the food, because she rarely eats it, sticking mainly to a liquid diet. Cocktails. It's the best summer holiday she's ever had. She just can't get over the thrilling idea that when you date waiters in America, you date Americans.

US/UK guide to naffness-avoidance: What not to do in each other's countries

AMERI-NAFF

When in the UK, don't:

1 buy china and Waterford crystal, then speak obsessively of the shipping charges for sending it home.
2 buy cashmere. Especially boring classics that are only $5 more in Gimbels.
3 buy tartans, or wear tartan berets in the streets because it makes you 'feel British'. Don't go into shops and insist on looking for your family tartan, especially if your name is Yablonsky.
4 talk about genealogy . . . yours or other people's. No one cares. You and everyone else you will meet are probably 7 billionth in line for the British throne. This is especially true if you are of Armenian descent.
5 talk about how 'civilized' London is. It isn't.
6 forget to stand on the right of escalators in tubes. It irritates natives.
7 be sycophantically complimentary about members of the Royal Family. It's creepy.
8 assume that people you meet would secretly like to trade places with you. They wouldn't. They like being British.

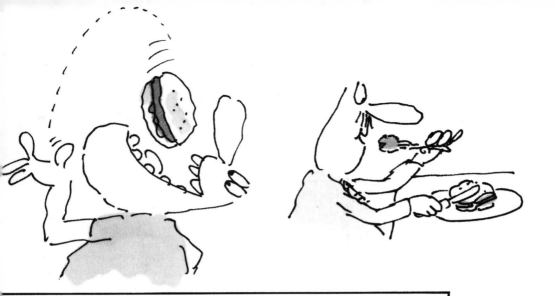

BRIT-NAFF

When in the US, don't:

1 eat hamburgers or sandwiches with a knife and fork. Even if they're huge and sloppy.
2 wear ankle-socks with sandals. Unless they're day-glo pink, and you're under 25.
3 insist that you only eat ice-cream in hot weather. Ice-cream is America's national dish. Temperature has nothing to do with it.
4 complain about the ubiquitous air-conditioning. (Take your cardy to restaurants and in cars.) Do not try to open the windows in skyscrapers for 'fresh air'. Ameri-windows do not open; Yanks prefer a 'controlled environment'.
5 remove the ice from drinks, or ask the waitress to leave it out so that you get more Coca Cola in the glass for your money.
6 be insulting about American television. You're already watching most of it at home.
7 wonder aloud how all the sunny days will affect plants (they have sprinkler systems) or how people get by without better public transport (they have cars).
8 call dessert 'pudding' . . . 'what's for pudding?' They won't understand, and they'll think *you're* one.

3 Strictly business

What George Bernard Shaw once said about men and women could apply equally well to British and American businessmen: 'They're destined never to understand each other, but doomed to forever try.' Take the hungry and hopeful Yank, resplendent in his flawless suit and matching manicure. He has failed to hoist one important psychological point, and it will prove his undoing: Brits are perverse, and respond badly to personal packaging. Perfect grooming strikes them as suspicious . . . slightly intimidating. They become wary of manipulation, and hence resistant to propositions. It is hard to trust someone who looks richer than you feel.

Corporate Yank who wants to start a productive dialogue must try to appear sympathetic. This means *human*, and even (here he'll have to work against the grain) *flawed*. OUT with zomboid corporate-speak. ELIMINATE phrases like, 'in Chicago, we're very excited about the new data-control operation . . . ' which sound nearly as plastic as 'have a nice day', and make Brit-eyes glaze over. Hair can be rumpled, shoes a bit scuffed. Suit should look lived in.

This is a hard lesson for Yanks to learn. Usual US business practice dictates that those trying to clinch deals must convey — in dress and demeanour — the impression that:

1 they have made money, and are therefore at ease with it, and
2 they treat it Very Seriously. Nothing on this planet is more important than The Deal.

There will be no sloppy mistakes. Perfect attire reassures others that you are equally immaculate in your thinking. (You have covered every wrinkle.)

It is not unknown for Brit associates to maroon a Yank in this very professionalism. It's a form of intellectual one-upmanship to suggest that 'of course it's important, Old Chap, but there's more to life than the bottom line'. There is, for example, the countryside, and Sunday lunch. Corporate Brit can't resist pricking the bubble of gung-ho-ness. It's a nasty trick, and visiting Yank reports back to Chicago that 'you can't talk to these people'.

The thing Brits hate most in Yank associates is their infernal *optimism*. This reads to them as the worst kind of naïvety. Brits often cultivate, for business purposes, the image of those who are world-weary with experience, and have been around all the houses at least once. There is a common reluctance to entertain new ideas, make special efforts, or ever miss the 5.46 home to Weybridge. Instead, one earns corporate Brownie-points for 'making the best of a bad job'.

Enter the fresh-faced Yank, brimming with enthusiasm and fiscal fitness. The Irresistible Force has met the Immovable Object. He's re-invented the wheel, and seems bent on talking about it. He comes on like a corporate adolescent as he rabbits about 'more cost-effective ways', and 'simpler solutions'. Brits have mixed emotions when they appear to work.

Succeeding in business

BRIT-THINK: A nation of shopkeepers it may be, but in the final analysis, Brits and business are spiritually incompatible. 'Business' is all about meeting the changing needs of consumers, and Brits loathe change. They especially hate *consumer-led* change, believing that the little sods ought to take what they can get and like it. Fortunately, British consumers are docile, not to say supine. They do not demand a liberal 'returns' policy in stores, and therefore are stuck with all purchases unless faulty. They will eat food in any combination pre-ordained by restaurants. They will accept prescriptions from doctors without asking simple questions about contents or side-effects, and — if damaged — will not sue. If they buy goods which break within short periods (the blade snaps on an electric blender, the washing-machine floods, the heel comes off a shoe) they will accept blame for having mis-used it. They are content to purchase all electrical appliances *minus* the plugs, thus involving themselves in extra expense and inconvenience.

The result is that British businessmen are drunk with power, and never give the suckers an even break. For years they have sold people ovens too small to cook a big turkey in, twin-tub 'automatic' washers which will not launder clothes without human intervention, refrigerators which require primitive defrosting methods, and teensy expensive sandwiches — which would not satisfy an anorexic in the last stages of decline.

Not surprisingly, British industry is — by American standards — shrouded in secrecy. For instance, it often displays a deep-rooted fear of the Press. It seems that British businessmen can't bear the idea of being *watched* while doing whatever it is that they do. This is probably because they can't *explain* whatever it is that they do ... except to say, 'we've always done it this way'.

Intimidation and desks

AMERI-THINK: The American office desk is a symbol of status and power, as is the waiting-time you — the supplicant — spend in the outer office before you *see* the desk. (NOTE: In Los Angeles — and especially in the film and television industry — a special formula applies, wherein the relative importance of the executive you're about to see is inversely proportionate to the waiting-time you spend in his outer office, and to his height — i.e., a two-hour wait should produce a man who is both impotent and short.)

However: the more senior the executive, the larger his desk; so, the Big Boss will sit behind a surface that a family of ten could live on for a year. Unless it's roughly the size of a platform at Calcutta railway station, it doesn't count. The point is that desks are Macho, and desks intimidate. They also protect ... interposing a beautifully grained and polished fortress between Big Boss and you.

You are placed at an instant disadvantage. First, you will have to shout across vast spaces in order to be heard. Big Boss will also ensure that your guest-chair is low, and the desk-rim level with your mouth. This gives him a chance to say 'What? Can you speak up? I can't hear!' until you are thoroughly rattled. Second — and most important — it places you too far away to judge whether Big Boss is stupid or smart. If he is seated behind his desk when you come in, you won't know if he's tall or short. Or thin or fat. You will not spot his contact lenses or recent hair implant. Or the fact that he's just had the bags beneath his eyes done.

The large desk will be housed in an equally impressive office, with breathtaking panoramas of city skyline beyond slimline venetian blinds, over shaded landscapes of plush carpet. It should look like J.R. Ewing's office, presided over by a Barbie-doll secretary who is also an acolyte. Already it's two against one.

BRIT-THINK: Brit executives understand intimidation, too — but their style is somewhat different. Surprisingly senior men — especially in the upper echelons of government and broadcasting — have scruffy offices with half-dead plants producing mutant stems on dusty window-sills. They bend over desks which appear to have been bought second-hand at an industrial close-out. The 'phones have dials, the typewriters are antiques, and so are some of the secretaries. The tea lady shrieks, 'tea, dear?' from the corridor each time she passes, and sloshes stewed brew into half-melted plastic cups. 'That'll be 7p, dear.'

In short, Brit-boss lacks glossy props. But (and this is important) he is on his Own Turf. Despite the seediness of the surroundings — or perhaps because of them — he hopes to project a sense of class . . . superior intellect, breeding and education, which — as every Brit knows — are perfectly consistent with being down-at-heel. Brit-boss has also been brought up to believe that a man in command can afford to underplay his hand.

Unfortunately, the pitch works only on other Brits. Visiting Yanks are not sufficiently conversant with the subtleties of the class-system to be impressed. What they see merely confuses them. They do not think about Oxbridge or the Corridors of Power or the Old Boys' Net. They simply return to the hotel and wonder why such a Big Cheese looks like a real Shlep.

4 Brits and Yanks at home

Home as backdrop

AMERI-THINK: The home is the ultimate expression of Me. It is one area over which I have perfect control; a place to display aspirations and live out fantasies ... however eclectic these may be. Home is multi-faceted Me.

There's a 'tropical' room with whirling ceiling fans and plenty of rattan; an English Tudor dining-room with hammered beams in the ceiling; an apricot-and-gilt bedroom where I've indulged my taste for Louis XVI, and a hi-tech post-modernist media room with faux-marbled walls. What matter if the exterior is red brick neo-Federalist, or Cape Cod shingle? If America is a cultural melting-pot, so is its domestic architecture ... as a quick drive through Beverly Hills will confirm. Forget consistency. It's *impact* we're after.

Members of the aspirational middle classes will have 'an interior decorator' as surely as they will have hairdressers, gynaecologists and 'day-workers' (cleaning ladies). The role of the decorator is not to 'impose' taste (surely not), but to 'interpret' the client's *life-style*. Ameri-clients will gladly pay the heftiest fees in return for the assurance that they *have* life-styles.

A good decorator can do much to mask personal shortcomings. Shaky taste can be 're-edited' into something acceptable; even a client who is a real slob can be cunningly re-packaged as 'California casual'. This means lots of scatter-cushions on the floor and Navajo blankets thrown casually over the backs of chairs so the mess looks intentional.

Yanks enjoy creating domestic scenarios ('home as backdrop') and are accustomed to shelling out proportionately. $5,000 per room, counting furniture and labour, is considered quite average. They redecorate houses from top-to-bottom every time they move ... and they move often. It's a rare Yank who's prepared to live with someone else's carpet or wallpaper. Not only does it cramp his style, but 'you never know what they've done on it'.

Ameri-home is the obvious physical expression of the American Dream. By Euro-standards, even yer average shack is 'super-equipped'. It has Kleenex in every room. It has air-conditioning, micro-waves, media centres, computerized security systems and automatic ice-cube dispensers. It has intercoms, piped gas barbeques, water-and-air purifiers, sprinkler systems and remote-controlled garage doors. Americans are probably the only people in the world who can't contemplate life without a built-in garbage compactor.

Home as bolt-hole ('Don't tell anyone I live here')

BRIT-THINK: There is beauty (and safety) in anonymity ... which may explain why middle-class dwellings from one end of the country to the other are nearly identical. Brits in every income-bracket short of the very top dislike domestic ostentation, and decline to call attention to their homes ('just so long as it's tidy'). They are happiest with formula floor-plans and 'traditional' features. From Washington New Town to Weybridge, proud owners peep from behind net curtains and leaded lights.

Round about the 1920s, a little-known architectural genius designed the first-ever bay-windowed semi-detached. A grateful nation has reproduced it ever since (with only minor modifications) from Cornwall to Aberdeen. It is etched on the nation's consciousness; felt to be the perfect dwelling, and the one which best suits and accommodates the British Way of Life. It is somehow 'right'. The only thing 'righter' is a (period) house in the country, if you can afford one. But flats are not right — nor are open-plan rooms, double-volume spaces, warm-air central-heating, soaring two-storey windows or radical design-statements. These are regarded as architectural perversions, which inevitably distort life within. Even the Prince of Wales gets publicly sarky every time he spots too much glass.

Brit-homes have no equipment at all. Somewhere in the backs of Brit-minds, an indoor loo-with-low-flush-mechanism is still perceived as a 'luxury' (the most over-used word in the estate agent's lexicon). The heating system doesn't work, though exposed radiators deface every wall-surface, and scald the cat. For reasons few can explain, Brits will spend many happy hours reading and talking in front of a false fireplace. (They are irresistibly drawn to any hint of neo-Georgian fibreboard surrounding an area of blank wall.) This is Spiritually Right, and re-inforces traditional family values. Home is where the hearth isn't.

Brits haven't much need for interior designers, since the last thing they're after is showiness, idiosyncrasy or display. (That's reserved for gardens and 'grounds'.) Only *two* decorative themes are allowable, and these are repeated the length and breadth of the nation:

1 *For the affluent, aspirational, or upwardly mobile:*
   The 'country house' style. This calls for a great deal of antique furniture ('repro' if you can't afford the real thing), dark woods (mahogany is favoured), gilded mirrors, floral fabrics and swagged velvets, well-worn Oriental rugs (nothing new, and *never* 'washed Chinese') and subdued colour-schemes. Anything, in fact, which looks inherited and suggests Old Money. Can be scruffy, since Old Money often is.

2 *For everyone else:*
   Post Second World War Ugly.
   Main design-feature is carpets, fabrics and wallpapers which jar horribly, and look as if they've ended up in the same room only because of 'shortages'. (Brit-style seems permanently circumscribed by the post-war period.) Favoured colour-schemes run to avocado-cream-brown, or alternatively black-with-orange blobs. Or both.

Time-honoured features and principles of Brit-design:

1 *Never buy new furniture*

   Furniture is something you replace only when the old stuff wears out ... never for aesthetic reasons. ('I know it's 30 years old, but it's a perfectly good couch.') When forced to buy new, choose something which looks old, thus re-inforcing links with family and tradition. When you move to a new house, take old pieces with you — however out-of-place they seem in new surroundings. Sentiment should outweigh other considerations. It is un-British to re-decorate from scratch.

2 *Find a focal point for your room*

   The false fireplace will do, or a 3-barred radiant heater, or a coffee table. Whatever you decide, this *must* (for lo, it is written) be surrounded by three pieces of furniture; one sofa and two chairs.

3 *Welcome to my nightmare*

   Choose furnishing patterns purely because you *like* them, and not because they complement each other. Brown and black swirls in the carpet, pastel roses on the wallpaper, art-Deco zig-zags in primary colours for the curtains. You know you've succeeded when you get car-sick just sitting on the sofa.

4 *Create carpet interest*

   Whatever you do, avoid running one carpet choice throughout the house. The various patterns are specially effective where they join at doorways.

5 *The importance of lighting*

   Opt for the subtlety of a single bulb, hanging on an exposed wire from the centre of the ceiling. For added interest, cover with fabric shade in bordello-red or cream. Control with hanging light cord. (Replace when grubby.) If forced to use wall light-switches, place high enough so that they can just be reached on tippy-toe.

6 *Accent with pictures ...*

   hung too high up the wall for anyone at ground-level to see without spraining neck-muscles. Then hang decorative mirror high on opposite wall, perfectly placed to reflect junction with ceiling.

7 *Every boudoir should have one*

There's a law somewhere in the Brit decorating canon which says that every bedroom must have a dressing-table. This must have a mirror which must be placed at a bedroom window, so that the unpainted back is visible from the street.

8 *Hole idea*

Brit kitchens suffer from condensation. Remedy this by punching a hole in the kitchen window, with primitive cover operated by dirty string. Ventilator itself will also attract dirt, cause uncomfortable draughts, and breed a whole new strain of Legionnaire's Disease. It will do nothing, however, to alleviate the condensation — which is caused by time-honoured Brit-building methods.

9 *No change*

Above all, your home must look and feel precisely like the one you grew up in. This is your chance to make time stand still. You may have an up-to-the-minute fashion sense, complete with magenta Mohican, but this will not extend to your surroundings, which Mummy will understand. Even Katherine Hamnett groupies still watch telly sitting on sage green dralon. All Brit-homes are clone homes.

Some like it hot

The greatest single difference between Brits and Yanks is in common perceptions of heat and cold. It seems that natives of each country possess internal thermometers — acquired at the moment of birth — which remain unchanged even if they spend many years abroad. Accents and attitudes may alter, but thermometers never do.

Americans are cold in Britain from the moment their planes touch down at Heathrow. They're cold outdoors, and even colder *in*. But they're coldest of all in the bathroom. There, their suffering is complete . . . largely because of the British predilection for failing to heat toilet areas, then throwing windows open in order to simulate latrine conditions. A sense of defecatory well-being is clearly considered decadent. (This has something to do with early potty-training by frosty nannies, and Spartan conditions in boarding-school or military service.) At any rate, most Brits are now accustomed to a state of chronic constipation. Desperate Yanks, used to cosier conditions and rather more roughage in the diet, have been known to pay volunteers to warm the seats for them.

Brits, while sympathetic at first, soon grow impatient with shivering Yanks, and advise them to wear more clothing. Americans pay scant attention. They hold the view that clothes are for aesthetic and fashion purposes only, and should not be required to do the job for which central heating was intended. They flatly refuse suggestions of thermal vests from Marks and Sparks. Primitive to don extra layers when you can push up a thermostat. Anyway — after years of wholemeal diets and 'working out with weights', who needs to look fat? So, they continue to huddle miserably by heaters, and soon reach the conclusion that the refrigerator is the only thing in the average British home which is never cold.

Brits on heat

When in America, many Brits show sudden concern for the environment, and accuse Yanks of squandering energy resources. This is because they are very uncomfortable inside buildings, felled by the white-hot blast of serious central heating. They complain that it makes them dopey, and dries out nasal passages. (No one knows why they prefer wet ones.)

In America, Brits first experience *uniform* heating, having typically spent formative years searching for the warm spots in cold rooms. Suddenly, they are *parched*. They throw open hotel windows in a desperate bid to re-create draughts. Bowls of water placed by the bed simulate the general air of dampness they associate with home. Brits can't sleep in a room where there's no condensation on the mattress.

In fact, they are not only *grumpy* in wrap-around central heating ... they are psychologically *distressed* by it. Heat, to be acceptable, must have a source — must be directional. For preference, it should come from the front (coal fires, gas or electric heaters) leaving your face flushed, your back and shoulders stiff and frozen. 'Proper' heat is something around which a normal family can group the three statutory pieces of furniture. Try that around a warm-air duct.

Ordeal by water

AMERI-THINK: It's a question of what turns you on, and what you turn on. Yanks believe that British bathrooms exist to mortify the flesh ... (some people *like* it). Icy loo seats, abrasive toilet-tissue, showers that don't work (inadequate water-pressure) or spray everywhere (hard water

Of course, the water will warm up slightly once you get in.

sediment's bunged up the holes). If you're lucky, you get a thin trickle — useless for washing shampoo out of hair, but perfect for flooding the floor. This is even easier when the shower curtain is missing. Brit bathrooms are not for sybarites. They are frosty places where one learns the true meaning of endurance. When the British Army wants to go on survival training exercises, it spends two or three nights in a British bathroom.

Then there are Great British Bath Taps. Brits practise a kind of lavatorial Apartheid; hot-and-cold taps are separated as far as porcelain will allow, with nary a warm-water mixer in sight. One tap is scalding, the other is ice-cold. It tests initiative to regulate the flow to produce a mix of the required degree of warmness. By the time you discover your bath's too cold, you'll have exhausted the supply of hot water.

Some help is at hand in the form of the new, hi-tech British mixer. This produces not *warm* water, but parallel streams of hot and cold running from the same tap. There are myriad possibilities for serious injury; and since spouts are placed as close to the sides of the basin as possible, it is virtually impossible to wet a toothbrush or fill a glass without risking collision.

Beddy-bye

Hardy Yanks who survive the rigours of a British bathroom and make it into bed are not home and dry. At least not *dry*. Apart from the dampness factor, there is the question of flatness. British beds aren't. The tops are stitched and tufted to make sure that:

1   you never enjoy a smooth night's sleep, and
2   lint of scientific interest gathers in the holes.

Traditional Brit-bedding is lumpy bedding. Furthermore, all-wool blankets of enormous hairiness are still preferred. They immobilize your legs under a great weight, and keep you in place — which is just as well, since Brit beds are very high, and if you roll out the fall can kill you.

American dreams

An American's bed attests to his personal style in the same way as his home ... and the more extravagant, the better. After all — it's a third of your life, and so on. Yanks sink their beds into carpeted platforms, hang them hammock-like on swinging chains, and install motors to make them tilt, revolve, and face the built-in media deck. Americans, too, have accidents while sleeping ... but only if the waterbed bursts, causing short-circuits in the quadrophonic sound system and halogen light-show.

Closet needs

Americans like their closets to sleep 4. All modern houses and apartments are supplied with spacious 'walk-ins', which allow your clothes to live in greater luxury than some people. Chances are that you'll also have large mirrors — even 3-way jobs — so that you can know the hideous truth about your rear end and trousers.

Brits have loads of clothing, but no closets. Old houses were built without them, and because 'we've always done it this way', today's builders see no reason to change. Instead, they extol the virtues of 'free-standing' wardrobes: 'gives you such flexibility when planning your bedroom!' What it really offers is greater expense (you have to buy the wardrobes) and decreased floor-space (the furniture takes up most of it).

Furthermore, Brit wardrobes are cunningly crafted to be a fraction less deep that the span of the average hanger when positioned on the rails. This means that the doors never close properly. The rail's so high that you can't reach it, and bows under the weight of even a few garments, allowing dresses and skirt-hems to hit the floor. (Brit wardrobe manufacturers look harshly upon people with more than three changes of outfit.) And judging from the provision of mirrors, these should be viewed from the front only — and from the knees up.

5 Choosing partners ...
'What's love got to do with it?'

First appearances

AMERI-THINK: 'If I've one life to live,' breathes a beauty in a famous American TV commercial, 'let me live it as a blonde!' As has been noted, it goes against the Ameri-grain to concede that 'we pass this way but once'. Just in case, however, true Yanks are determined to make the most of it. Appearance is vital. Suggest that beauty is only skin-deep, or that character counts most, and natural scepticism overwhelms them. It's all very well to have a fab. personality; but — if you want to reach for the stars (and every American does) — you'll also need straight teeth.

They're equally pragmatic about nature and its wondrousness. 'If nature's blown it, we'll fix it' is the national *cri-de-coeur* that's launched a million cosmetic operations. It's clear that the quality of your life — and your enjoyment of it — is largely dependent on the way you look. There's little doubt that appearance affects popularity, and financial success. 'Just as God Made Me' is not always good enough. Look what He did with earwigs.

Ironically, Yanks — with most of life's basic necessities under wraps — are the world's greatest malcontents. They seek perfection, and cannot rest until they've made the best of a bad job. Every bad job. When it comes to themselves and their personal prospects, no effort is too great, no correction or refinement too insignificant, no orthodontist too expensive. Americans invest in themselves happily, guiltlessly. After all — when life is so precious, why waste a single day feeling bad about your nose?

This is the blessing and the curse of American affluence. If everything's possible, and no real obstructions stand in your way, you've no excuses. Failure is your fault. So is unhappiness.

BRIT-THINK: Nature usually gets it right the first time. Think carefully before pressing the 'over-ride' button. There's no such thing as perfection in this less-than-perfect world, and humans are no exception to the rule. What *is* success, anyway? How can you measure it, and what matter if you don't achieve it? Does British society respect you less if you're poor? (Yes.) Penalize you if you're stupid? (Of course.) Discriminate against you if you're unattractive? (Right on.)

To seek perfection is to commit the sin of hubris. Brits are fatalists ... 'we all die anyway'. Why suffer and sacrifice for an uncertain (and inevitably temporary) gain? It is enough just to· Be. Avoid tampering, or trying too hard, which is unbecoming. Anyway — the class system gives you a natural place in the scheme of things. If you like, it's yours for life.

Yanks may believe that self-improvement = upward mobility = progress ... but Brits hate the idea. For one thing, it suggests *change*. For another, it encourages a burst of personal initiative ... your fate in your own hands, and so on. That idea makes Brits very tired. 'Let It Be', sang Paul McCartney.

That goes for things physical as well. Why spend good money to straighten little Jeremy's peculiar teeth? Pure indulgence, when all mortals are flawed. If you're going to lash out, invest in something sensible — like a new music centre.

Mouths

'Fed up to the typically English teeth'

BRIT-THINK: Brits have some of the most curious dental configurations in the world. Their mouths often appear too small for a normal number of teeth. Anglo-orifices are tiny and discreet, nestling unobtrusively between nose and chin ... (Mick Jagger's mouth is not orificially British). Brits keep stiff upper lips because they do not wish to call attention to their mouths by moving them. Large, wet, mobile apertures (like Mick's) strike them as obscene. Besides, they are hiding their teeth, since dental problems are woefully neglected. If there's one thing that frightens Brits more than the prospect of change, it's dentists.

AMERI-THINK: Ameri-mouths are more generous, and usually open. This accounts for the difference between British and American *sandwiches*. Brits are forced to nibble thin cucumber ones because their mouths don't open wide enough to accommodate American whoppers. Ameri-jaws will separate at an angle of 180 degrees, no problem. Bring on the pastrami.

Let's Get Physical: Evolution of the Yank Species

Physical perfection is supremely important in the selection of an Ameri-mate. First-class *appearance* is a reliable indicator of:

1. Intelligence. (You're smart enough to take care of your body.)
2. Self-esteem. (You like yourself well enough to want to.)
3. Affluence. (The peak condition of the thoroughbred can, to a large extent, be bought.)
4. Good genes. (Your biological inheritance.) Chances are that your progenitors were *also* all of the above. Ameri-masterpieces like you are no accident; they take generations to evolve.

In America, where there is no formal class-structure, fine physical appearance is a near-substitute. It's a mark of quality much sought-after when Yanks wish to marry 'up'. In top American dynasties, family members seem to be uniformly smart, rich, and *beautiful*. Look at the Kennedys; a perfect example of selective breeding if ever there was one. Ditto Hollywood and 'media' families. The litters produce few runts. Several generations of generous liquid assets, combined with heightened awareness of health and beauty (laced with public admiration), have produced beautiful parents producing beautiful children. And so Henry Fonda begat Jane, and Grace Kelly begat Princess Caroline, and Ernest Hemingway produced Margaux and Mariel, and Robert Mitchum several little Mitchums, and Edgar Bergen Candice, and so on. It seems to Americans that the very rich and famous are smart enough to be beautiful. What's luck got to do with it?

Mere mortals can only gasp, and imitate. This has led to a quest for physical perfection seldom seen since the days of Ancient Greece. Such is the popularity of health and beauty clubs, that every new condo and place of work must have one. The national fixation with weight-training, exercise, bran-products and stretch-lycra in assorted colours continues. Yuppies have deserted fashionable metropolitan singles bars, and seek romance in private gyms. This is because:

1 Cocktails are high in calories and destroy both brain-cells and Yuppie prospects.
2 The Mr Right you meet at the rowing machine will have a high muscle-to-fat ratio, and a long life-expectancy. Also, the price of membership to the gym.

Recognized signs to others that you are at the peak of physical condition, and therefore a desirable 'catch', include:

1 Straight teeth. Also, *white* teeth. Any discolouration can be interpreted as nicotine stains.

2 Tight stomach muscles. When lying on your back, a wooden ruler should rest on both your hip-bones without touching tummy. Flab is shmo.
3 A clear complexion (the outward sign of healthy eating), combined with well-conditioned hair which *moves* ... (the $30 cut).
4 Matching manicure. (See below).

The importance of fingernails

Brits don't understand this. 'Perfect down to the fingertips' is the main idea. All-American girls used to file theirs to graceful points, but no more. Experts on fingernail fitness decree that the sides are necessary for strength, and nail-structure improves if you square them off at the tops. Best physical specimens now have squared-off talons which attest to $30 manicures and $60 nail-wraps.

Yank-ettes flash them a great deal when talking. They tap things for emphasis: table-tops, wine-glasses, passages in newspapers, TV screens. They gesture extravagantly with their hands (why spend $30 if no one notices?). They eat tons of gelatine for healthy nails (outward signs of a sound body), and when one breaks, it spoils the whole day. When they get engaged, their husbands-to-be (transfixed by their fingers) buy large diamond solitaires to set them off. These are cheap by comparison to the on-going expense of nail-care.

Brit engagement rings

As comedienne Joan Rivers once said, staring incredulously at the third finger on a woman's left hand, 'you *married* the guy who gave you that puny little ring?' Most Brits feel it's fine for tokens of affection to be *modest*. (NOTE: the Princess of Wales was not taken in by this one; when Charles offered his heart, she also collected a £50,000 sapphire.) Generally, Brits persist in the notion that love has nothing to do with money ... that there's risk that the former will be vulgarized by the latter.

Eschewing ostentation as they do, even those with plenty of family lolly to spend will prefer:

1 Granny's inherited Victorian engagement ring
2 an antique engagement ring that *looks* like an inherited one
3 a new engagement ring of antique design

... to something modern and showy. If American taste runs to *rocks* like car headlights, Brit-bride chooses a discreet cluster of mixed stones (traditionally diamonds with sapphires or rubies), each pin-prick gemette weighing in at .00001 carat, and nearly invisible to the naked eye. The ring is a maze of little platinum struts, topped with the merest hint of sparkle.

As a symbol, it's perfect. It's so clearly tasteful ... like love. And personal. Like love. And sweet. Like love. And disappointing. Like love.

Ameri-rocks ... (Ring as deposit)

The point is that Yankee brides *mistrust* small stones. The groom's investment in a ring is a deposit — an act of faith. It indicates that:

1   He cares. (He has adorned your body with something expensive.)
2   He intends to stay with you. (Your ring has absorbed all his run-money.)
3   He wants the best for you, so that:
4   He will work his socks off to make it all happen.

It's part of a marital pact; a question of mutual commitment and — perhaps more important — aspiration. A flashy ring is a symbol of your husband's intention to SUCCEED, and be a good provider. A puny ring is a symbol of his intention to stay a shlep.

6 Aspirations . . . or, 'You can't have everything — where would you put it?'

'Having It All'

AMERI-THINK: Life is about 'Having It All' — the most American of catch-phrases. For years Yanks went around parroting well-worn clichés like, 'You Can't Have Everything'. But somewhere between the Fifties and the Eighties they changed their minds. Post-war Baby-Boomers — possibly the most influential members of society — now believe that you not only *can*, but *should* have it all: beauty, intelligence, ability, money, health — and fame as a result. The catch is that nothing happens unless you *make* it happen. Hence, the compulsion to exercise, diet, wheel-and-deal, write books, appear on talk shows, and marry 'up'. Also to live for ever, since there's scant time for total success in one lifetime. Even TV commercials appeal to the Yank's sense of comprehensive ambition; the slogan for low-cal beer *Michelob Light* runs, 'Oh Yes, You *Can* Have It All!'

Recent changes in television shows document the shift in attitudes. Three of today's brand-leaders are *Dallas*, *Dynasty*, and *Falconcrest* — serials depicting the world of the super-rich. Their popularity suggests that the American Dream has been up-graded . . . from the sweet, suburban comforts depicted in *Father Knows Best*, *Ozzie and Harriet*, and *Life of Riley*, to hard-core mega-wealth and all its privileges — including the freedom to be nasty. The Carringtons are fascinating because they let Americans see why and how the rich are different.

New American role-models are those who fend for themselves ('Rambo') and get their own way. 'Go for it!' is the buzz-word. People who've taken the idea to heart include athletes, rock-stars, models, businessmen, newscasters, and even TV weathermen. Many enjoy huge incomes, and convince themselves that 'I deserve it'. The syndicated television series, *Lifestyles of the Rich and Famous*, illustrates the material rewards of Me-think, and is a runaway success. Problem is that the possibility of 'Having It All' is a mixed blessing. Many Americans are now restless ... confused about how best to invest their energies. The question on nearly 250 million pairs of lips is, 'if it's all within reach, if I can have it all — why haven't I *got* it? How can I get it? And when is enough enough?'

Muddling through

Brits feel no desire to 'Have It All'. They were so relieved to learn that 'you can't have everything'. They prefer to relax, and enjoy working within life's natural boundaries — 'I'm not very good at games' — instead of kicking against them. As a nation, they are so fond of limitation, that where necessary, they will invent one: 'you're not the type to wear red'; 'he's not well suited to business'.

Brits hate being required to hustle and change the course of destiny —even in their own interests. They have a great and easy capacity for contentment, and can derive much satisfaction from small successes: 'look, dear, I've cleaned the fish-pond.' It's not — as is often said — that they are lazy. But they've seen the future, and decided that it doesn't work, and is not worth getting hot and bothered about. They are united in the belief that most change is neither possible nor desirable ... which also rules out improvement. So, Brits of all classes live for the moment. They have no master-plan, no ultimate ambition: 'What's it all about, Alfie?' As a group, they are a bit chaotic. It is a particularly British concept to 'muddle through'.

This distinguishes them from Yanks, who are in every sense goal-orientated ... 'I always do 27 lengths before breakfast'/'I want to be a millionaire before I'm 40.' In general, Brits are less single-minded and determined. Their private aspirations — if they can be identified, since they embarrass Brits — are more modest: 'this year, Muriel, I'll wipe out the greenfly.'

Historically, Brits have been wary of men of driving ambition ('that's how you get dictators. Or Scargill'). It's a romantic notion, anyway, for any one of us to think we can change the world. Silly to believe there's a reason why our own interests should prevail. That way lies ruin ... look at the Second World War. Far better to relax, and cultivate your own garden. Anything for a quiet life.

Yanks want to know why we're here. They're desperate to leave a mark on life, to impose some order on the chaos. They need to decide if it's all about money, or power, or love, and act accordingly. Brits *know* why we're here. In the words of the song, 'we're here because we're here'.

46

Brit soap

If the formula for American soap opera is high-life and success, Brits prefer low-life and failure. As Yanks sit transfixed by the private lives of oil tycoons, Brits dwell on the meagre surroundings of the socially deprived. Hence, the continuing popularity of *Coronation Street*, and *East Enders*. If the glossy images and fantasies peddled in *Dallas* and *Dynasty* are gratifying to one side, long-running sagas of grinding poverty are just as compelling to the other. Brits seem to find them soothing. They provide proof — if any is needed — that most men lead lives of quiet desperation; nasty, brutish and short. They match the national pessimism about:

1 things changing for the better
2 things changing at all.

Yanks find it thrilling to think there are yet more dizzying heights to achieve; Brits find it comforting to know that there's always someone worse off than *you* are.

Strike it rich

It follows that Americans generally want to, while Brits aren't that bothered. A favourite T-shirt, often seen on the streets of Manhattan, encapsulates Yank-think. It reads, 'Whoever Has The Most Things When He Dies Wins'. In the absence of other criteria for success, goods and assets will do. Life is very nearly quantifiable in cash terms. For instance: Yanks have never really believed that 'money won't buy health'. No one who's had dealings with the American medical profession would swallow that. As smart old Jimmy Durante once said: 'I've been rich . . . and I've been poor. And rich is better.'

BRIT-THINK: In 1985, when the pound was in crisis and sliding disastrously against the dollar, President Reagan said of the British: 'I think they have a way to go in changing some rigidities in their customs and methods of doing business.' This endeared him to few, and made it clear that his ignorance of Brit-think is complete. Little does he know that Brits cherish the 'rigidities' in the system, and seek to preserve them . . . that they do *not* sincerely want to be rich. (Well, not that much, anyway. Wouldn't say no to a win on the pools.) Such an idea is entirely outside his experience, and as outlandish as suddenly being told that Nancy has an obesity problem.

47

No: Britain is not a failed version of the US financial model. It fails on it's *own* terms. The structure is a dead weight, bearing down equally on the 'Them' side and the 'Us' side, ensuring paralysis and a certain symmetry. To Yank amazement, the British public seems content, and will vote in huge numbers for any Party promising not to change a thing.

Success story

Double standards

BRIT-THINK: Generally, Brits feel that to succeed — especially in financial terms — is, proportionately, to deprive someone else. They see society's resources as finite, so too great a concentration in individual hands is greedy and anti-social. This perception is not exclusive to Socialists, but is often shared by those on the political right: 'we-think'. Achievement must be tempered with a sense of social responsibility. Brits don't like piggies, and will unite in condemnation of anyone suspected of trying to corner a market.

Brit-censure does *not* extend to high-profile figures awash with *inherited* wealth. Even the poorest of the poor feel no resentment for the Queen or Royal Family, with their vast (tax-free) incomes and estates. This is because it's not the Queen's *fault* that she is rich. God knows, she didn't try, and it's probably a worry to her. (Heavy lies the head that controls the Crown Estates.)

Self-made men are admired (Sir Freddie Laker, Sir Clive Sinclair) as long as they don't push things too far (*folie de grandeur*). Brits are pessimists, believing that many a reach for the stars ends in a fall to earth. They often warm more to heroes on the way down (Sir Freddie Laker). Ideally, achievement should appear effortless. Success — unless it's somewhat fortuitous — can look grubby and gauche. Failure is at very least decorous, and rather dignified. *Cosier* than unmitigated success.

Nothing succeeds like success

AMERI-THINK: ... which is only *one* of the catch-phrases relating to success. Others include: Having It All/You've come a long way, baby/You're only as good as your last picture/All that counts is the bottom line. Success is literal, tangible. It usually brings material rewards. You can't be

48

successful in a vacuum since success must be apparent, and recognized by all. There are exceptions ('I'm a good mother') — though, to be frank, Americans find self-proclaimed success less convincing.

Yanks have no problem with the ambitious, or financially acquisitive. Society's resources (like its opportunities) are infinite; therefore, you can climb to the highest heights without appreciably harming me. There's plenty for everyone, more for smart guys. Moral: be a smart guy.

Americans favour a pragmatic approach to success. Do what you have to do as long as:

     1 it's legal, and
     2 it works.

When it *stops* working, get out quick with a blanket over your head. Yanks have little patience for failure.

Failure: Anglo-American excuses

Making dramas out of crises

BRIT-THINK: Since no one expects things to work, they are very tolerant of explanations for why they haven't. 'It can't be helped,' they shrug, resigned. Brits like things that can't be helped. The weather, for example. Or train derailments. Or power-failures, or national strikes. They are very fond of Acts of God — or indeed any situation which allows them to 'soldier on', vowing to 'muddle through somehow'. Brit Brownie-points for 'making the best of a bad job'. (This of course relieves you of any obligation to do a *good* one.)

Brits are adept at making the most of even minor setbacks. Because they have so few natural catastrophes on a grand scale (earthquakes, typhoons, volcanos, blizzards), they've learned to make full use of the ones they've got. The whole nation grinds to a halt because of delays in first-class postal services. Or points failure on Southern Region.

When business fails to profit, Brits are glad to accept 'acts of God' explanations. The problem is not poor planning, or woeful decisions; it's the unexpected rise in interest rates/devaluation of the Yen/ monsoons in Sri Lanka/collapse in oil prices. Less is mentioned of inaccurate research, failure to predict trends or contain damage. It's 'victim syndrome' — otherwise known as BRITVIC. Ask a Brit what he wants to be when he grows up, and the honest answer is 'a victim of circumstances'.

Delegating blame: 'It's 'a notta my fault!'

A UK press report on the Queen's visit to California commented on the ugliness and inappropriateness of one be-ribboned evening dress in the official wardrobe. 'In choosing it,' the journalist concluded, 'the Queen was badly advised.' IT'S 'A NOTTA HER FAULT!' She was but a passive victim, unable to influence events. Never let it be said that Her Majesty made an error of judgement. Off with a minion's head.

Brits are masters at delegating blame, which is why 'advisors' are so handy. Royal families seem to have zillions. In all walks of life 'professional advice' is highly regarded, and generally deferred to. In this way individuals are separated from the responsibility for their own decisions. 'Counsel' tells you whether or not to bring a court case, and you seldom seek a second opinion. Nor do you question 'professional' judgement: 'the doctor booked me in for an operation/teacher says Trevor's not university material/my bank manager told me I'd be able to afford the payments.' There's no need to do something difficult — like

The reason I'm successful Miss Mc Michael is that I know how to delegate blame.

think. Your fate is in someone else's hands. That way, there's always someone to behead when things go wrong.

AMERI-THINK: Americans only *pretend* to delegate. Anything. As Harry S. Truman once said, 'the buck stops here'. They suffer from a pathological fear of 'losing control', and a paranoid suspicion that, given a half-a-chance, others will 'screw you up'. Or at least treat your interests more casually than they would their own.

They're happiest keeping a firm grip on events, and asking a lot of questions. It's the boss's job to choose the right advisors, and his fault if they goof. (This is occasionally true in Britain as well, but only in the case of politicians — where a Ministerial *faux pas* can bring down the Government — or in football, when the team loses games and the Manager gets sacked.)

Yanks adore results, and have scant interest in the rationale for failure. They do not consider it ruthless to discard something — or someone — that hasn't worked. There's little sympathy for 'bad luck', or even 'Acts of God'. Furthermore, Yanks do not believe in 'accident'. There is simply no such thing, and here they are hard-boiled. 'You should've seen it coming. You should've been better prepared.' The Reagan administration took enormous flack for failing to anticipate suicide bomber attacks on US Marines in Beirut.

Fault is always attributable. Occasionally, there are such things as extenuating circumstances ('I fired in self-defence') but, in general, mainstream Yank-think sees most excuses as lame ones. 'I was knocked unconscious at the material time.' No good. You should've been more alert, or in better physical shape. Yanks associate failure with malingering ... or crass stupidity. Either way, they don't like being taken for a ride. And they don't like paying for what they don't get.

So who gets credit for *success*? A good business decision for example, or a wise choice of girl-friend/boy-friend or employee? You do, of course — because there's no such thing as 'accident'. If you are merely lucky, you will nevertheless be declared 'smart'. And how do you know when something's worked well? You know when someone else tells you. *Anyone* else. In general, Yanks lack confidence in their own tastes and decisions, and long to know that all choices are officially 'approved'. (Hence the popularity of Gucci belts, initial scarves, Nike sports shoes, Burberry raincoats and designer jeans.) It follows that a good decision is one that's *endorsed*. Even if it's by someone who's just as big a cluck as you.

51

Bouncing back

Recovery from adversity

BRIT-THINK: Brits don't. The perpetuation of problems is a point of some national pride. Never quit when you're on a losing roll. Heroism is about the struggle against adversity ... the triumph over it merely a footnote. Take the Second World War. Nice to win it of course; but the most gratifying part was the bit about holding out with courage and dignity.

In fact, so uncomfortable are Brits with real victory, that they have spent the past 40 years trying to redress the balance. Thanks to their unstinting efforts, the prime-movers on the losing side now enjoy far healthier economies than Britain's.

Set-backs

It is good form — and a mark of attractive humility — to be properly set back by set-backs. Small ones will do. This is not a nation of bouncers-back; all obstacles are regarded as major, all defeats as permanent. So people will entertain, as serious propositions, any of the following: 'He was never the same after his plumbing business collapsed.' 'Her life was ruined when she had to go to court on that parking charge, and then her daughter got divorced.' 'It finished her off when the corner laundrette closed down.'

In short, Yanks accept few excuses for failure, but see no reason why you can't begin anew. As often as necessary. There *is* life after defeat. Brits accept many reasons for failure, but seem determined to go down with their ships. This is because they do not fully believe in the possibility of fresh starts. Something in the national temperament makes them reject alternatives, and forego second chances. The Captain of the *Titanic* stood stoically on the bridge as she sank, murmuring, 'be British!'

This is even colder than my bathroom...

The ones that don't translate

. . . A collection of words and phrases totally misunderstood by the other side.

1 It ain't half hot (Brit. 1) = If anything isn't half anything, it means very something; i.e., if you're not half beautiful, you're gorgeous. Not surprisingly, a lot of Yanks don't understand this.

2 fancy (Brit. 1) = want, desire, lust after. The way British women feel about, say, Harrison Ford.
(Yank 1) = the opposite of plain. Frilly, decorated, with lots of things attached to it.
(could also apply to Harrison Ford.)

3 keen (Brit. 1) = totally sold on. Anxious to have. The way British men are supposed to feel about cricket.
(Yank 1) = sharp. A keen wit, for example.
(Yank 2) = preceded by 'neatsy', means "really fab".
Arcane usage found only in *Archie Annual* comic books, or primitive reaches of the San Fernando Valley.

4 roundabout (Brit. 1) = merrygoround; i.e., magic roundabout
(Brit. 2) = a circle of traffic where all normal rules of motoring are suspended. It is speculated that Brits have created them in preference to ordinary intersections so that:
(a) they can let off steam by dicing with death
(b) they can go around in circles, making a small country seem larger.

5 naff (Brit. 1) = in poor taste. A combination of vulgar, clichéd and tacky. MUSAK in restaurants is naff. Wearing designer-labels that show is naff. Liking Mantovani is naff, buying Cabbage Patch dolls is naff, men in open-necked shirts revealing chunky gold jewellery is naff, making your own yogurt is naff, sporting a T-shirt that reads RELAX is now naff. Things get naff fairly quickly, and as soon as they become clichés. Naff has no precise American equivalent, but should be used much more, since Yanks are hyper-conscious of naffness in all its forms. These days, it is pretty naff not to know the meaning of naff.

6 turkey	(Brit. 1)	= a feathered game bird too large to fit into the average British oven. Served and eaten at Christmas *ad nauseam*, but at no other time.
	(Yank 1)	= a jerk. A dodo, a real loser. Fair description of most of the guys you date at college.
	(Yank 2)	= Business-speak. The real thing; money. Usually preceded by the words, 'let's talk'.
7 out to lunch	(Brit. 1)	= where all people in business and service industries are between 11 a.m. (half-an-hour after they arrive at work) and 3.30 p.m. (half-an-hour before they break for tea).
	(Yank 1)	= Loony. Flakey, empty-headed, brainless. Possibly drug-crazed. At any rate, not there when you knock. May describe as much as half the population of greater Los Angeles.
8 making it	(Brit. 1)	= a form of DIY feminine = learning to crochet. masculine = carpentry made easy.
	(Yank 1)	= measurement of success. Financially speaking, income tops $100,000 a year.
	(Yank 2)	= sexual act. May describe *other* half of the population of greater Los Angeles.

7 The food connection

BRIT-CHOMP: Here, Brits have a problem with pure pleasure. They feel guilty about wallowing in food, like continental types; one should eat to live, and not the other way around. The traditional British diet reflects this sense of gastronomic utilitarianism. It runs to cold pork pie, sausages, offal (heart, tripe, braised kidney), zillions of things on toast (meat paste/cheese/baked beans/spaghetti) and zillions of permutations on the general theme of mince (i.e., shepherd's pie). The best thing that can be said for this sort of Brit-fare is that, in the short term, it keeps you alive. In the long term, it probably kills you.

Though Brits are slowly becoming more diet-and-health conscious (bearing in mind their natural resistance to change), many food favourites bear more relation to solid fuel than nutrition as we know it. It must be remembered that middle-aged Brits grew up in the post-war years, with their legacy of basic food shortages and ration-books. An egg was a luxury, many fruits and vegetables scarce. But there were heavy syrup puddings, and cakes made with lard. Mum needed two strong men and a fork-lift truck to remove baked goods from the oven.

Eating in Britain: Things that confuse American tourists

1 Why do Brits like snacks that combine *two starches*?
  (a) If you've got spaghetti, do you really need the toast?
  (b) What's a 'chip-butty'? Is it fatal?
2 Why is British pie-crust removed from the oven while the dough is still raw and white?
3 Is bread-with-dripping a form of mass suicide which involves voluntarily clogging your own arteries?
4 Is cockaleekie the curse of the permissive society?

5   What is Marmite? What are Ribena and Lucozade? What is their connection with the British Way of Life and the War Effort?
6   Why are they nuts about Weetabix ... the only breakfast cereal designed to disintegrate into mush on first contact with milk?
7   Why do they call cake 'gateau'? Why is the icing on a birthday-gateau hard and thick enough to prevent nuclear melt-down?
8   Sandwich, huh? I see the bread ... but where's the filling?
9   What have they got against water?
10 What have they got against ice-cubes?
11 Is that why the beer is warm?
12 What this town needs is a good coffee shop.
13 What is a 'stone'? How many do I weigh? How about *after* I eat the pork pie?

Most Brits are not very experimental about food. They won't touch anything that they haven't eaten since earliest childhood ... ('if Mum didn't serve it, I don't want it'). This leaves them with a very limited range, which includes toast soldiers and orange squash. There are those who consider spaghetti bolognese and pizza exotic ... 'foreign muck'. Years spent at the mercy of Mum and/or a succession of school cooks have made them wary of consuming plant-life (i.e., all fruit and veg.) in its natural state. When confronted with a raw vegetable, they will revert to earliest training and boil it for hours to make sure it is dead. Indirectly, this is the reason for the Spartan nature of British bathrooms. Brits never need to use them.

AMERI-SLURP: Most Yanks are heavily into food. Up to the elbows, if possible. If they like something, they don't so much *eat* it, as *merge* with it. Basically, their tastes are simple: hamburgers, pizza, ice cream with hot fudge. Huge, mouth-watering hunks of cheesecake topped with whole strawberries. Also — things that remind them of the range and variety of America's ethnic heritage — kolbasi, strudel, lasagne, gefilte fish, pastrami. Together if possible.

As in interior decor, Yanks are open-minded about combinations. After all, they invented the 'combination sandwich'. (Where else can you get a corned beef, pastrami and breast of turkey combo, with melted cheese, cole slaw and Russian dressing on rye?) Nevertheless, they draw the line at anything too authentic. Culinary tradition is diverse, but carefully adapted to American tastes ... Yanks have a way of sanitizing

food. Wiener schnitzel may sell in a German restaurant, but not the blood sausage. Ditto kebabs in a Greek establishment, but not the whole baby octopus. Bland, processed 'American' cheese is popular, but the powerful French varieties virtually unknown. Though America produces some of the world's best wines, more consumers prefer Coke.

Yanks like to be shielded from the realities of eating — and cooking. This is, after all, the nation that invented the pop-up toaster waffle and frozen orange juice. Butcher shops and supermarkets are careful never to let a customer see a whole animal — nothing to associate their selections with life on the hoof. (Most Americans think that meat grows in polystyrene and cling-film.) They tamper with liquor to mix the world's best cocktails — and with grain to produce the most revolting breakfast cereals. The world has Yanks to thank for sugar-and-honey-coated Cocoa Puffs.

The importance of sharing

Americans don't just *eat* food — they participate in it. No where else will a total stranger pass your restaurant table, glance at your plate, and ask, 'is it good?' Eating is a shared experience. Ameri-male in love cannot take his eyes from his girl-friend's face — or his fork from her plate. True love is never having to ask permission.

Friends and relatives do the same, with a tangle of anxious arms criss-crossing the table and spearing food in all directions. Brits are put right off, seeing this as an invasion of privacy and disgusting as well. When visiting America, they live in fear that a casual acquaintance or business associate may ask to taste something of theirs. Should they treat it as a presumptuous intimacy, or a friendly gesture? Does it constitute a binding contract? How can you negotiate tough terms with someone who has your hot fudge all over his face?

Because America is made for sharing, portions come in giant sizes ... usually enough for two or three. Waitresses will provide extra plates without batting an eyelid ... though, recently, some maverick establishments have introduced 'sharing charges'. These are seen as a threat to the American way of life.

In case dividing the lobster, or the spare ribs, or the onion-ring loaf is messy, plastic bibs and extra napkins are provided. It is OK, even *de rigueur* in these circumstances, to behave like a slob. The waitress will eventually come around to ask if you're enjoying your dinner. It will be hard to answer with a full mouth.

American children visit restaurants from earliest infancy, and share their mothers' dinners. At the age of 6, they need dinners of their own, because they eat more than she does. Brit-kids are not generally 'taken out' — unless you count fast-food take aways, or the occasional tea-shop treat. It is considered that they need different diets than adults, and thrive best on a meal called 'nursery tea' ... which is specially composed to include 100 per cent carbohydrate, and no protein at all. Biscuits, cake, bread-and-butter, crisps and spaghetti-on-toast are favourites, and these must be consumed:

1 in the company of other children, or at most one adult (mum or nanny). Brits operate strict rules of nutritional Apartheid.

2 at 5 p.m. latest.
   Brit-kids retire early, and are not allowed to:
      (a) stay up 'til 9
      (b) eat with grown-ups
      (c) eat real food
      ... until they are 26.

Hence, the evolution of Britain's most popular children's classics. Peter Pan was not a 'lost boy' who never grew up. He was a child with protein deficiency whose growth was stunted.

Brit guide to Ameri-portions

1 **Char-broiled New York cut steak** (8–13 oz)
will overhang the plate on one side. Share with friend.

2 **Prime ribs of beef**
will overhang the plate on both sides. Ask for *two* extra side-dishes to take overspill.

3 **Surf-and-turf** (combo. of lobster-tail and steak)
won't fit on the plate in the first place. Served on special wooden stay-hot griddle platter. You won't need dessert.

4 **Onion-loaf** (side order only)
feeds four generously, six adequately. Ignore waitress advice that you need one for every two people.

5 **Club sandwich**
... not quite big enough for the whole club. Divide with one child.

6 **Salad (spinach, waldorf, Caesar, fruit)**
contains world's natural reserves of raw fruit and veg. Undoes benefits of low calories if you eat it all. Share with one other weight-watcher.

7 **Banana split**
three can share. One scoop per person. Child gets the cherry.

8 **Ice cream cone (any size)**
no one can share. It's too good, and each person will want it all. It is not unusual for a grown-up to come to blows with a child over an outstanding cone.

8 The political divide

Brit-body-politic:

The Great Political Divide (see p. 14) governs everything that happens (or doesn't) in Britain. Because loyalties are polarized, all attitudes are partisan ... so *every* issue is a political one. Say 'ham sandwich', and you'll discover that there are two sides to the story. No doubt a debate about ham sandwiches is part of the on-going political dialogue. Only Brits can immediately see the relevance of luncheon meat to the Party Manifesto/Industrial Relations Bill/social contract/welfare state/free market economy/central borrowing requirement.

Party Manifestos (US = 'Platforms')

Because Brits are convinced that there are so many important — and distinct — choices to be made, they treat Party Manifestos *very seriously*. These are blueprints for action during a term of office, wherein Party intentions are spelt out. This way, voters aren't 'buying blind'. Manifestos are studied carefully, referred to frequently by news commentators, and felt to constitute a kind of contract with the electorate. Any failure to live up to obligations is seen as a breach of same.

    'Manifestos' are known as 'Party platforms' in America, where they are fodder for the waste-paper basket. Or the shredder. Few things have less credibility than campaign promises, whether they are written down or not. When made orally, they are certainly not worth the paper they're not written on.

    Anyway, 'policy' — of any kind — is now recognized as the biggest vote-loser of all time. Who'd want one? (See Reagan victory, November 1984.) In Britain, the Social Democrats are just beginning to catch on.

Party political broadcasts

In both countries, absolute and total nadir in the art of communication. Brits prefer a 'morning assembly'-style school lecture, where a senior member of the Party in question (usually the ugliest Cabinet Minister they can find) is allowed to harangue the electorate for five uninterrupted minutes in prime TV time. Brit Party-politicals are technologically primitive. The camera does an imperceptibly slow zoom *in*, seldom cutting away from the hectoring mug which fills the screen — except to pick up pre-recorded snatches of conversation with the converted, the deprived or the demented, who have 10 seconds apiece in which to whinge about the opposition. This is called Vox Pops.

Then, cut back to Big Daddy, now in hard close-up, each eyebrow measuring six inches across. He is instructing us slowly, patiently — as he would a class of nursery children — on our patriotic duty to vote for him. In simple words. So that we can understand. Brit politicians have a way of addressing the electorate as if it were collectively under sedation.

US politicians use every trick in the technological book to produce a commercial of which Madison Avenue can be proud. The result owes much to Hollywood, and not a little to MTV. The product — (Prexy-to-be) — looks so *good*. The wind ruffles his hair so playfully. The sun glances off his best side as he stands by the seashore, and sparkles in the centres of his eyes. He seems alert, capable. Dissolves and filters keep him looking young, vibrant, even *sexy*. With luck, no one need ever know that he is clinically dead.

He doesn't spend much time speaking directly to the punters, though the Party Political records brief snatches of his finest — or most endearing — moments at public occasions. If he has ever made a joke, been shot or wounded in the course of public duty (impaled on a fork during a fund-raising luncheon) it will be recalled here. Assassination attempts are run in slow motion. A voice-over intones the campaign slogan meant to stick in the minds of voters: 'America's Back' . . . or, 'Leadership That Is Working'. But the *pièce de résistance* is always a shameless piece of emotional manipulation at the epi-centre of the party political. The candidate will be seen in the Great Outdoors, romping playfully with his devoted wife, family (corralled for the occasion), dogs, and — if possible — a selection of ethnically diverse Ameri-kids. Or ethnically diverse veterans from the Armed Forces. Or both.

62

The thorny question of Class

> Me daughter says you're an 'upwardly mobile' gentleman, though frankly I think the two things are irreconcilable.

Gotta Lotta Class

BRIT-THINK: Brits have more class (and class distinctions) than any country in the world with the possible exception of India. This is why the two nations reached a certain understanding during the period of the Raj; in some respects, they have much in common. Even today, questions of British caste, income and voting patterns are oriental in their complexity.

Outsiders can seldom be taught. You have to be born British to understand, to grasp the nuances. Sometimes, it's just a lilt in the voice.

There are, however, perceptible voting patterns which are some clue to class and social status. Yanks may be helped by the following guidelines:

If you are a Brit, you will vote Labour IF:

... you see yourself as bottom half of the eco-pile, identify with salaried workers rather than bosses or the self-employed, question the beauty of the Capitalist system, support the extension of the Welfare

63

State, and — more generally — the redistribution of resources from 'Haves' to 'Have Nots'.

You are doubtful about:

1   the wisdom of Anglo-American nuclear policy,
2   support for the Israeli cause,
3   the objectivity of the Brit 'Tory' press ...
     'pro-Yank, biased against Russia, Conservative Party lackies.'

If you are a Brit, you will vote Conservative IF:

... you instinctively group yourself with society's 'winners', see yourself as upwardly mobile, feel that, on balance, the present Capitalist system represents the best of all possible worlds. You identify your personal interests as bound up with the 'Establishment', feel impatient with welfare spending, sceptical about public ownership, and generally anxious to ensure the survival of the status quo until you get where you're going.

If you are a Brit, you will vote Liberal, SDP, or SDP-Lib. Alliance IF:

.... you're all of the latter (see Conservative voters) but conscience-stricken about the poor and less educated, obsessed with marginal libertarian issues ('a better deal for remand prisoners', 'compulsory seat belts for rear-seat passengers'), confused about defence, living in a nice residential area, a regular *Guardian* reader, and richer than nine-tenths of all Conservative voters.

There is one more category of Brit voter worth noting. Known as 'deferential Conservatives', these are people of modest means with no real power-base and no significant stake in the system, who could normally be expected to vote Labour. But they don't. They vote Tory because:

1   their mothers and fathers did,
2   they have confidence in the system, plus an abiding and deferential respect for the clever people who run it,
3   they don't like to be any trouble to anyone.

Deferential Conservatives know that they're not going anywhere, but they don't seem to mind. They accept their place in the general scheme of things. Anyway, 'better the devil you know' and so on. Deferentials are phobic about change. Some political analysts claim that *all* Brits are deferential Conservatives at heart.

Sons and daughters of deferential Conservatives often display a tendency to cross over in the opposite political direction. This is specially true if their parents' modest but unstinting efforts have provided them with tertiary education. They are Britain's equivalent of Yuppies (Buppies?) and have bright futures, but are somewhat crippled by an emotional dilemma. They see their parents as wimps and victims, but can't face the trauma of despising them. Instead, they turn upon the (Conservative) system which emasculated them, and develop serious social consciences. This means that they wear jeans and hush-puppies, study law but decline to practise, vote Labour and go to work for the BBC. There they spend the rest of their natural lives making hard-hitting documentaries about the perils of multi-lateralism/atrocities of British troops in Northern Ireland/Nelson Mandela, and eventually end up as Heads of Department.

Class Act

AMERI-SNOB: In Britain, voting-patterns are fairly reliable indicators of 'class'. Stateside, it ain't necessarily so. Therefore, American is commonly billed as 'the Classless Society'. Not true! Yanks are every bit as status-conscious as Brits. The difference is that, in America, class is not something you're born with, but something you can achieve. It has less to do with heritage than *impact*. Americans think that Joan Collins has class.

They are also terrific snobs. 'Class' — as Brits understand it — is about your past. Snobbery is about *now*. To Yanks, it's about places you don't want to be seen in, cars you won't drive, places you never shop, life-styles you don't want to have. It's about the right addresses, restaurants, clubs, hotels. Because Yank-society is so fluid, you can move to a new town — or even neighbourhood — and 'create yourself in your own image'. You can constantly up-date, and if necessary, custom-design a New You. Yanks do this meticulously, in a thousand different ways. Personal development is an important key to social mobility. Choices you make must be the right ones. You must look good, live well, project successfulness if you want to pass muster. So Yanks think carefully about points of style. A Class Act in America is a triumph of form over content.

As in all things, Yanks are prepared to work much harder at class than Brits, whose place in the hierarchy is immutable, and guaranteed — removing all need to keep up appearances. Which is why many top Brits feel perfectly entitled — with a touch of reverse snobbery — to be perfect scruffs.

Yanks pay the price for unlimited social mobility. If British birthright is a trap, it is also secure, obviating the need to prove anything. One Just Is. Yanks, in their anxiety to define themselves, grasp at straws — or Cartier tank watches, or Gucci reversible belts. Status-symbols are class. Money is class. Spending it stylishly is classiest of all. Yank-snob knows that suburban living in Connecticut is class, but New Jersey isn't. Ownership of virtually any apartment in Manhattan is now class. Driving a Jag or a Mercedes is class, but an (equally expensive) flashy white Cadillac isn't. A condo in Palm Beach is class, one down the coast at Lauderdale isn't. Shopping for discount clothes at Loehmann's can be class, J.C. Penney's never. You can take the kids to McDonald's for hamburgers and still have class — but if you eat there without them, you've blown it.

Ameri-snob is also unforgiving. Because he is self-made, he demands the same initiative from others. Because his expectations are high, he has no time for shmos. Because in America anything is possible, he has no patience for failures. Including his own.

Yanks are terribly hard on themselves. If you *can* do it, it follows that you *should* do it . . . no excuses allowed. And there's very little room for human frailty, few allowable shortcomings. If you're fat, you must also be stupid. At any rate, *fat* is not *class*. Increasingly, Yanks are perfectionists.

9 The importance of being 'cute'

AMERI-THINK: To succeed in America, you have to be 'cute'. This should be interpreted in its broadest sense, and is — in Ameri-minds — very nearly a Metaphysical concept. It refers not just to endearing children (though it helps to start early if you want to get the hang of it). Cute also means arresting, appealing, charismatic and satisfying. Spiritually, you are vibrating at the same frequency as Ameri-culture. This is the true meaning of success.

Anyone, anything, and any *idea* can be called cute — so the term is lavishly applied. New-born babies are cute, Doppler radar is cute, Tom Selleck is cute, and so are Star Wars technology, raspberry popcorn, lots of sit-coms and selected restaurants. Even serious corporations can get cute. An astute American businesswoman called Meg decided to name her financial consultancy 'Meg-a-bucks'.

'Cute' scratches a national itch. It describes everything you want someone (or something) to be. Cute is instant gratification, and wish-fulfilment. It has about it the delight of a fantasy-come-true. Presidents can be cute . . . virtually *have* to be video-cute in order to win. President Kennedy was very, very cute and he knew it. He was a national turn-on. Cute-looking, cute personality and cuter sense of humour. Remember how cute he was when he arrived on his first Presidential visit to France, and greeted cheering crowds with, 'Hello. I'm the man who accompanied Jackie Kennedy to Paris'? At times, it seemed he could do no wrong. Even Congress thought he was cute, which was important after the Bay of Pigs fiasco, which wasn't so cute. He was allowed to redeem himself with a successful conclusion to the Cuban missile crisis, which was pretty cute.

Many world leaders (including President Reagan but not Mrs Thatcher) have drawn important lessons from this. The charm bred of gently self-mocking self-awareness — especially when deployed by public figures — is unstoppable. It works for the young, and for geriatrics. And if you're cute enough, you can have anything. America is up for grabs.

BRIT-THINK: The importance of being cute is only dimly perceived by Brits, with the possible exception of Robert Morley. Most British politicos, though, have miles to go before they can be considered fully humanoid, never mind seductive and appealing. Neil Kinnock has instinctive charm and the potential to be cute . . . but Mrs T. has *no* self-awareness, and cannot make her loyalest voters fall in love. Dr David Owen wastes a nice face, since he is far too severe and brittle a personality to be cute. Ken Livingstone is kinda cute, and nearly overplays it. It would be hard to find senior politicians less cute than Norman Tebbit and Sir Geoffrey Howe. President Reagan knows how to be cute (and little else). Nixon knew everything else, but wasn't a bit cute. Henry Kissinger could be cute-ish when he put his considerable mind to it. Cap. Weinberger is not one of life's natural cuties.

Of course, it is possible to be well-known and successful without being cute. But latest scientifically-designed 'cuteness-factor' research shows than canny cuties surface faster — and get rich quicker. Here's the latest dip-stick poll on Anglo-American cuteness:

AMERI-CUTE:

Goldie Hawn is so cute you could throw up.

Ditto Liza Minelli and Drew Barrymore.

Ronald Reagan is cute.

Nancy isn't.

Ron and Nancy together are perceived as 'cute' by those Americans who like watching senior citizens hold hands.

There are people who think John McEnroe is cute.

There is no one who thinks Jimmy Connors is.

Bruce Springsteen does not like being considered 'cute', but when you are worth a hundred zillion dollars, you substitute cuteness for credibility.

BRIT-CUTE:

The Queen and Prince Philip are far too grand to be 'cute' together in public. This is because they are not required to win elections.

Mrs T. doesn't comprehend the importance of being cute.

Dennis does, but M. cramps his style.

Cecil Parkinson was too cute for his own good.

Terry Wogan is Irish and cute.

Michael Aspel is English and cute.

Clive James is Australian and cute, if you like it a touch vicious.

Prince Charles is cute, ears notwithstanding. Could be even cuter if he'd let himself. If you are rich and Royal, it is nearly impossible not to be *devastatingly* cute ... but, because he is square, he has managed.

Brits often dismiss cuteness as intellectually crass. It is merely another form of Ameri-hype, to which finer minds are immune. Brit-feelings run deeper, and their spirits are far less easily galvanized (only by the Royal Family, Bob Geldof, First Division football clubs, or any mention of the Second World War). Yanks, on the other hand, can be aroused by almost anything. An emotional bumper-sticker. A pom pom display by the Dallas Cowboys' cheerleaders.

Unless restrained, Americans take cuteness to saccharine extremes ... ('Shirley Temple syndrome'). Only they could tolerate the spectacle of Ron and Nancy walking hand-in-hand into a Republican sunset. Or invent Coca Cola corporate ads. Or thrill to the beauty secrets of Linda Evans, or sit through syndicated repeats of 'The Love Boat'.

But Brits shouldn't feel smug. They have their own version of surrender to popular myth, and it's called 'cosy-ness'. As a state-of-mind, it's just as inert and self-congratulatory as cuteness. It is wholesale, blanket satisfaction with all things British ... a kind of institutionalized self-love. Cosiness is centrally generated by the BBC, which postulates a national attitude with every minute of air-time, daring people to depart from it. The Beeb is honour, goodness and truth. The Beeb is family, the Civil Service and the Queen. The Beeb is ... Us. How cosy.

If cuteness fills Ameri-hearts with optimism, so does cosiness arouse self-esteem in Brits. It promotes a sense of uniqueness, worth, and particular charm: 'There are no others like us', 'Brit is Beautiful', 'Nobody Does It Better'. This conveniently reinforces the status quo, since cosiness contains no suggestion of the need for change.

Loving the Royal Family is fundamentally cosy. The two-week observance of Brit-Christmas is cosy. Gardening is cosy, forming orderly queues at the slightest provocation is cosy ... (Brits pride themselves on waiting their turn in all things). Most news coverage is excruciatingly cosy, dwelling on the detritus of Brit-life at the expense of the larger, international story. Island-think.

All this contributes to an exceptionally cosy self-image. Brits see themselves as well-behaved people; honourable, fair-minded and moderate. This in spite of years of class division, colonial rule, industrial strife and football hooliganism. Cosy ideas are those which support this perception — especially at the expense of other 'less well-behaved' nations.

Other cosy things Brits do

1 Extol the amateur

Brits dislike anything too slick or professional, on the grounds that: (a) it demands an appropriate response, and (b) indicates that someone has been breaking faith by Trying Hard. This is rather a betrayal of the Gents' Agreement that 'we don't go for the throat, old chap, there's room for everyone.' Brits are disconcerted by evidence that, behind their backs, someone has been playing to win. Because competition of a serious, professional nature is frowned upon, Brits have invented cricket, where the real objective is breaking for tea and sandwiches.

2 Obstruct MPs

Parliament is still seen by many as an adventure playground for adults with time on their hands and independent means. Brits attempt to ensure that only benevolent duffers run for office by refusing to treat requirements seriously. For instance, they

    1 deprive back-benchers of a living wage.

    2 deny them reasonable office facilities. (It is felt that they can work adequately two to a desk, and twenty-five to a urinal.)

3 refuse funds for decent secretarial services. Parliamentary secs are often well-born young ladies whose derisory wages are subsidized by parental largesse. This arrangement underpins the entire British Parliamentary system.

3 Fill their national newspapers with 'Around America' columns

These are reports from a correspondent somewhere in the US, which invariably portray New York, or LA, or Texas as violent, anarchic and bizarre — ('Houston Man Marries Snake') — thus pandering to the UK reader's (and editor's) desire to see Britain as the last bastion of sanity in a flakey world. All very cosy. Stories pose the tacit proposition that social breakdown is the inevitable consequence of Not Being British.

4 Cultivate their gardens

Brit-Man is born with a unique, atavistic reflex, hitherto unrecorded by medical science. From birth, he has the ability to grasp a garden trowel. An allotment is a Brit's ultimate expression of cosy amateurishness. His garden is the domaine of his soul, and not for the incursions of others. So he will mow his own lawn, saw branches off trees, dig, trim and sow ... even if he is wealthy enough to afford an army of gardeners. No one knows why. He claims that the exercise is good for him (though he wouldn't dream of jogging, swimming, or taking any other kind) and so prunes and hoes to the point of coronary arrest.

In all this, he is cheered on by a Brit-wife born with an understanding of his need to dig. The same urge stirs in her loins. She knows that there's something about gardening which is British, and 'right' — which is the same thing as cosy. Doesn't matter what the interior of the house looks like, as long as the garden is 'right'. Then, life is 'right', and Britain is 'right', and the threat of greenfly is the only blot on the horizon.

10 Regionalism and other local problems

AMERI-THINK: America has five main regions:

1 *The East*

In theory, this means the Eastern Seaboard states. But what *really* counts is the New York City/Washington/Boston megapolitan area, combined with certain prosperous suburbs in Connecticut, White Plains, northern New Jersey, eastern Pennsylvania, Long Island and eastern Massachusetts.

2 *The West*

For 'West', read: greater Los Angeles, San Francisco, Marin County, Palm Springs, Scottsdale and La Jolla. Maybe Denver, but no one knew it was there until *Dynasty*.

3 *The South*

i.e., Atlanta, Miami and New Orleans.

4 *Texas*

i.e., Texas.

5 *The Midwest*

i.e., everywhere else. For purposes of this classification, Maine is spiritually the Midwest. So is Kansas. So is Tucson. Chicago is the high spot, but because it is in the Midwest, few people yearn to live there.

Nothing which is unlisted counts, and only two of the areas above count *heavily*: 1 and 2 (Sorry, Texas). Forget conversations you've heard about rural roots, and respect for America's heartland ... (i.e., the Midwest). Forget songs about going back to Swanee and midnight trains to Georgia; ditto received wisdom about the recent boom in the Sunshine Belt. Forget publicity about Pittsburgh being the most 'liveable' city in the United States, or Seattle the most beautiful. Most of all, forget

72

comments about New York being a nice place to visit, but nobody wanting to live there. Secretly, EVERY American wants to live there — or in Los Angeles. That's why they all pack up and go there, just as soon as they grow up. Because New York and LA are still perceived as 'best' (Sorry, Texas) and the best is what every true American wants to experience. At least once. So he can say he's been.

Until a few years ago this bias towards the coasts and away from the middle (neatly summed up in the famous *New Yorker* cover) was also reflected in television programmes. The vast majority used New York or LA as locations — notable exceptions being *Surfside 6* (Miami), *Hawaii 5-0* (Honolulu), and *The Walton Family* (even if Appalachia never looked like that). Then, with *Dallas* as ground breaker, TV moguls discovered the allure of the regions, and became more adventurous about settings . . . though choices were made with care. *Dallas* probably wouldn't've made it as 'Lubbock'. *The Dukes of Hazard*, well-situated in Jimmy Carter's Georgia, might've lost appeal in rural Alabama, or southern Missouri. Pretty soon, moguls screwed up courage to boldly go where no one but ski-buffs had gone before. Denver. Whatever next . . . Wheeling? Altoona?

The point is that America's got magnets at both ends, which exert a powerful draw, and cause epic movements of peoples to opposite sides. You'd think it would droop at the edges. But Americans take the constant shifting and displacement in stride. It does not appear to provoke undue rivalry, or resentment. Sure, Californians wish Midwesterners would stay out of the San Fernando Valley long enough to steady sky-rocketing house prices. OK, southerners think New York City spends extravagantly on welfare, and ought not to be bailed out with Federal funds. Yes, New Yorkers with 52 bolts on their apartment doors slate Texans who take a handgun when they nip down to the 7-11. (Sorry, Texas.) And certainly, there are racial issues (like busing) which cut across regional ones. But, for the most part, specific *regional* differences have not been a burning obsession since Appomattox. Michigan has nothing against Arkansas. And there's no question of devolution for Texas. Sorry, Texas.

BRIT-THINK: Britain is, of course, much smaller in terms of area — but regional differences are legion ... as well as complex and occasionally explosive (Ulster being only one manifestation). Baffled Yanks should picture an area roughly the size of Pennsylvania, divided into eleven distinct and potentially warring parts, some of which threaten to devolve from the rest, and from time-to-time shoot it out in London. Britain is:

1 Scotland
2 Wales
3 Ulster
4 The Republic of Ireland
5 The West Country (Cornwall, Devon, Somerset)
6 The North (Manchester, Liverpool, Leeds)
7 The North-east (Newcastle-Upon-Tyne and the rest of Geordie-land)
8 The Midlands (Birmingham)
9 East Anglia
10 The South (The Home Counties and similar commuterland)
11 Central London

Each area considers itself unique. Each feels it has certain irreconcilable differences with the rest of Britain. Each lays claim to characteristics so important and distinct, that they must be:

1 acknowledged as 'special' by the rest of the nation, and
2 preserved — in all their idiosyncratic glory — at any cost.

74

It is hard for Americans to believe, but Yorkshire and Lancashire —
which share a common border and many cultural similarities — are
hotbeds of local animosity over perceived differences. It has something
to do with different recipes for Yorkshire pudding.

Curiously, for people who identify so closely with regions of origin,
Brits refuse to tell outsiders where they're from. Two Yanks who meet for
the first time will greet each other with, 'Hi. Where're you from?'
'Chicago,' comes the casual answer. Or 'Cleveland'. Nothing heavy. But,
try it on a Brit, and watch the harmless ice-breaker cause a Big Chill.
Instead of replying simply, 'London', or 'Manchester', he freezes,
tongue-tied. You have intruded, somehow, on private matters, and
embarrassed him. If he answers at all, he'll make do with an evasive, 'oh,
the South'. Hard to come back with, 'hey! I knew somebody on your
street'.

This reaction is hard to explain, except to say that — as ever — it has something to do with class-consciousness. Pieces of basic (and apparently neutral) data like

1 birthplace
2 father's job
3 school attended

are felt to define status, and make Brits feel exposed. Even (or especially) if your companion has a fine pedigree and an Oxbridge degree, wild horses won't drag it from him/her. Not until you know each other well. There's a ring of truth to the old joke, 'Never ask an Englishman where he's from. If he's from Yorkshire, he'll tell you; and if not, it's unfair to embarrass him.'

On a less personal level, 'preserving regional differences' is an important cultural concept to Brits . . . though no one knows why. If you pressed them, they would cite differences in accent or phraseology, unique methods of thatching a roof, local varieties of cheese or sausages. That's about it, really. But regional loyalties are felt as deeply in East Anglia as in volatile Northern Ireland, and such things are taken seriously.

It seems that Brits have a kind of primeval fear of being 'homogenized' — culturally swamped — first by each other, and then by America. They regard as a threat the slightest 'foreign' influence: 'We don't say *"movies"* here in Scunthorpe. That's an American word. We say *films.'* Or: 'This is Britain. We don't celebrate Valentine's Day or Hallowe'en.' They often reject the mores and influence of London: 'This is a nice, quiet town. We don't like to go out to night-clubs like Londoners'; 'We can't be doing with all that central heating . . . we like our coal fires'; 'We eat lunch at mid-day and a proper tea, not that fast-food rubbish.' Regional die-hards feel culturally threatened by the growth of McDonald's.

Much of this is incomprehensible to Yanks, who may think of themselves as 'southerners' or 'midwesterners', but spend little time contemplating the Minnesotan nature of Minnesota, as compared, say, to Wisconsin. Perceiving yourself as a 'Scot' or a 'Welshman' presupposes a different level of emotional involvement than 'hailing from New Jersey'. One reason, of course, is that Americans move around much more than Brits, and regional loyalties are fudged accordingly. In an age when Concorde crosses the Atlantic at the speed of sound, it's hard to believe that generations of Brit-families feel spiritually bound to the immediate environs of Barnsley. Remember Michael Palin's line in the Python film, *Jabberwocky*. Sent off (for the first time in his 22 years) from his native village to one 3 miles down the road, he enthuses, 'Oh, good. I've always wanted to travel.'

Interestingly, the fierce loyalty that Brits feel for regions is reserved by Yanks for cities. Many a heart beats for the Big Apple and all it can offer. So passionately do they love their cities (even the most unprepossessing) that they are moved to sing great songs about them. If you have ever had a look at Amarillo, you will surely wonder why anyone ever wanted to be shown the way to it.

Brits, on the other hand, seldom croon about metropolitan locations, though they are sometimes inspired by the countryside ... 'White Cliffs of Dover', 'How Are Things In Glochamoragh?' (On second thought, that was probably composed in America.) It's certainly significant that, endowed with a city as unique and spectacular as London, the best they have recently managed is the downbeat 'A Foggy Day In London Town'. Lacks the exhilaration of ' ... start spreadin' the news ... I'm leaving today ... .'

Anyway, Yanks have proved that love is blind, and when you're besotted enough, you can sing about anything. Bruce Springsteen even managed one about Asbury Park, New Jersey. Other famous US city songs include:

NEW YORK, NEW YORK (It's a helluva town)
NEW YORK, NEW YORK (So good they named it twice)
NEW YORK, NEW YORK (I wanna be a part of it) *as adapted by British Caledonian
CHICAGO, CHICAGO (That toddlin' town)
SAN FRANCISCO (I left my heart in)
PHOENIX (By the time I get to)
SAN JOSE (Do you know the way to)
TULSA (I was only twenty-four hours from)
AMARILLO (Show me the way to)
MIAMI (Moon over)
KANSAS CITY (Everything's up to date in)
PITTSBURGH (There's a pawnshop on a corner in)
ST LOUIS (Meet me in)

... and so on.

There are even ditties about the allure of industrial agglomerations like 'Union City New Jersey', 'Galveston', and 'Gary, Indiana'. But, call to

77

mind if you can a song about Birmingham, or Leeds or Liverpool. (Yes, but that was Little Jimmy Osmond.) Or CROYDON. Maybe it's just that nothing in this world rhymes with Croydon. Try it.

The Neasden connection ... Place-names

Like songs about cities, British place-names tend to lack pizzaz. Somehow, there's little grandeur, or emotional impact. Consider, for instance, GRIMSBY. Scunthorpe/Neasden/Blackpool/Frinton-on-Sea. TWICKENHAM, for heaven's sake. What could sound more earthbound? Not for Brits the heart-swelling euphony of a 'San Francisco'. And it's doubtful that Tim Rice and Andrew Lloyd Webber would've scored a world-wide mega-hit with 'Don't Cry For Me, Hemel Hempstead'.

No: Brits like to live in places that sound — here it is again — cosy. Even if they have industrial blight and teeming populations. 'Newcastle-Upon-Tyne'. Sounds pretty, doesn't it? 'Swansea'.

If Brits reside in small villages (their true spiritual homes) they prefer place-names redolent of Olde Worlde Charme. These are cosier-than-cosy ... by definition, 'twee' ... evoking warming visions of thatch-on-roof, copper-on-walls, roses-on-trellis, scones-in-fireplace, and woodworm-in-beams. Consider Nether Wallop, Little Didcot, things in-the-Marsh, things on-the-Wold, and things under-Lyme. And if that's not cosy enough, Brits assign names to their cottage homes and rural hideaways. Yes, if great estates and palaces can have titles (Sandringham, Blenheim), why not your retirement bungalow? This is a harmless device for allowing Brits from all walks of life to live out the 'country house' fantasy. Patient postmen find their way to thousands of Lake Views, Shangri-La's and Journey's Ends.

Of course, the cosiness of the British landscape — decorously arranged on human scale — contributes to the snugness of it all. Nowhere in these Sceptred Isles are Brits outfaced by their own topography; nature has the decency to behave. There are no towering mountain-ranges, no deserts, no glaciers, no natural wonders (unless you count Hadrian's Wall, and he was Italian). And if a mischievous Providence *had* placed Mt Everest somewhere in Britain, chances are that the natives would have called it 'Perriwinkle Tor'.

11 At one with nature

BRIT-NATURE ... Like the people, it knows its place, and is sensibly understated. Nothing vulgar and tasteless, lavish or splashy. No great geysers or volcanoes, jungles or waterfalls. Hills keep a low profile, embarrassed to be mountains, and splodge around instead camouflaged as heather-covered lumps. Nothing is out of scale. Not for rural England the OTT extravagance of a Mt St Helens, or a Niagara Falls or a Grand Canyon. A Brit's idea of a canyon is when the Gas Board digs up the mains.

BACK TO NATURE
AMERI-STYLE

I love nature, know what I mean on weekdays Glady's and I just have to get out of the city for a breather she's crazy about flowers, any kind, and the food really tastes different I mean vegetables with no chemical spray or Agent Orange or whatever that stuff is I love the wilds where you're really at one with nature ever been to Cape Cod cook your own steamers right on the beach or back-packing in the Adirondacks great for the kids not far from Ho Jo's motor lodge if you need a shower. Last year we really roughed it $400 a night for your own log cabin in the Rockies accessible only by private helicopter no telephones no TV you should see the personalised bath robes first time I ever ate bear meat did you know its very low in saturated fats of course if it were up to me I'd rent a condo in Fort Lauderdale where theres absolutely nothing between you and the sea ....

To Yanks, the countryside (serious, hard-core countryside) is not for *living* in (not during the week, anyway) unless you're a farmer, mountain man, or vestigial member of a hippie commune. After all, isolation can be dangerous, and self-imposed isolation is contributory negligence. Anyone who wanders too far from major urban hospitals with full medical facilities deserves what he gets.

Brit-idyll:

Every Brit — even if he comes from an inner-urban area like Shoreditch — is born with a deep longing for the countryside which is coded in his genes. This is the rural idyll. If he's forced to live and work in town, the yearning goes unsatisfied until retirement, when — seized by some primitive instinct — he 'ups sticks' and moves to a seaside town he's never seen before.

Secretly, every Brit wishes he had 'independent means' which would enable him to spend his whole life in the country. He sees himself as Benevolent Squire or Lord of the Manor ... because, to be landed and well-born, and own dogs and family silver and be photographed by Lichfield in a Burberry raincoat is to every Brit the apogee of existence.

Failing the whole and perfect fantasy, he settles for a reasonable approximation. He buys the raincoat. Also, a neo-Tudor home 'with grounds' in a green-belt suburb. Or a weekend country cottage, where he can live — for two days anyway — in a non-competitive environment in contented squalor. An Englishman's compost heap is the ultimate expression of his understanding of the 'quality of life'.

The more unblemished his hideaway by traces of twentieth-century life (like working plumbing) the better. He and his wife will poke obsessively at innocent bits of soil for up to twelve hours a day. His crop of home-grown sprouts testifies to the fact that he is free ... beholden to no man. He is aided and abetted by the cosiness, the sheer reliability of British weather. It is sure to rain. However, he need fear no earthquakes, monsoons, hurricanes or droughts. Even the animals are on his side (animals are *always* on a Brit's side, and vice versa). (See 'Pets,' p. 139.) There are virtually no poisonous snakes, no sting-rays or tarantulas or rogue elephants. Statistics show that few people are savaged by sheep ... but, in any case, sudden death seems less important when one is at one with nature. (Which is just as well, considering the calibre of rural hospitals.)

Glossary (and translation) of Anglo-American weather terms

AMER.

spring —
three months between mid-March and mid-June when you put your winter coat away.

summer —
when you turn on the air-conditioning.

drought —
crops die. Animals in danger. Water-reserves low. Dust-bowl time.

hot —
high 70s Fahrenheit, upwards.

unbearable —
scorcher. 100 degrees F.

blizzard —
snow drifts to several feet, traffic stops, snow-plows come out. New Yorkers wear aprè-ski boots in streets.

you won't need your sweater —
it's T-shirt weather. Expect 80s–90s F, no rain, no wind.

you won't need your umbrella —
forecast predicts no rain. Hasn't been any for a week. Anyway, we'll be in the car.

BRIT.

spring —
a time when you switch off all forms of central heating, but it remains as cold as January.

summer —
the rain gets warmer.

drought —
two consecutive days without downpour.

hot —
a glimmer of light appears between cloud masses. The entire British nation strips to the waist. Term also describes the interior temperature of any room which has all the windows closed.

unbearable —
low 70s F, or more than ten minutes in the room with the windows closed.

blizzard —
slush on pavements. Traffic comes to standstill. Points failure on Southern Region.

you won't need your sweater —
no one has died of exposure overnight. (Yanks hearing this advice from a Brit should ignore it. It does not apply to them, and may be harmful to health.)

you won't need your umbrella —
speaker is either:
(a) impersonating a Brit (True Brits never move without their brollies), or
(b) no longer in Britain.

12 Patriotism ... crazy for the Red, White and Blue

AMERI-THINK: PATRIOTISM = prime example of the Ameri-adage that anything worth doing is worth overdoing. High-schmaltz factor. Another word for 'team spirit', best and most satisfyingly demonstrated at dazzling half-time intervals during pro-football games, at the opening ceremony of the LA Olympics, or by singing the 'Star-Spangled Banner' before the first pitch at the World Series.

Patriotism is slick, flamboyant, gushing and sentimental as a Diana Ross concert ... which explains why it's inextricably linked in the Ameri-mind with Show-Biz and Hollywood. And no wonder, in a country where movie stars become Presidents, and — in Jerry Ford's case — vice versa. There's also some confusion about Robert Redford and Jimmy Stewart.

Hollywood-style production is applied to State occasions, Presidential campaigns, inaugural ceremonies, and ticker-tape parades for astronauts. National sports fixtures and the Miss America Pageant have quasi-patriotic status. TV celebrations of historic events (for example, the 1976 Bi-centennial) are marked by 'spectaculars' which turn out hundreds of veteran stars, who aren't sure if they're celebrating the greatness of Hollywood, the greatness of America, or the greatness of having 'made it' in America. Goldie Hawn or Cher or Liza Minelli usually appear to breathe a few cute words of Holly-wisdom into a microphone; Frank Sinatra and Helen Reddy sing an emotionally charged number directly to the President; and Bob Hope arrives hot-foot from a golf-game with him ... at which point, all distinctions between Show-Biz and patriotism blur. Most Americans believe that the annual Oscar Ceremony is a patriotic event. (Marlon Brando certainly does.)

Yank stomachs are strong enough for the most banal public displays. When it comes to patriotism, they seem able to tolerate anything — however contrived or mawkish: an emotional 'phone call from the President to the mother of a dead hero — her tears, his 'God bless you' —

is networked coast-to-coast; so is a 'mercy flight', where the First Lady escorts charming third-world children to America for vital medical care. U.S.-style patriotism is elaborately stage-managed, and everyone knows it ... politicians, Press, even the dimmest voters. Strangely, few protest. Even the sharpest commentators seem loathe to blow the gaffe — perhaps because Americans enjoy the show, and they're all on the same side anyway. So, they allow themselves a spasm or two of patriotic rapture. Haute-schmaltz re-kindles the national sense of optimism, and there are no penalty-points for wallowing. JFK used to telephone Judy Garland, just so she could sing 'Over The Rainbow' down the wires to him. It kept him happy.

Yanks remain unselfconscious about Euro-impressions of such displays. They consider that — for the richest and most powerful nation on earth — they are models of restraint ... (like Brits, they see themselves as a well-behaved nation). They speak softly, and carry a big stick. They don't flaunt their superiority, but act with tact and care internationally. They don't flex their muscles or rough people up for the hell of it. Unless you count Grenadans. No: when you've got it, they reason, you don't have to flaunt it.

Problem is that they expect others — especially their NATO allies — to share their good opinion of themselves. When 'friends' fail to do so, they are deeply hurt, and feel betrayed. It follows that Yanks spend a lot of time feeling hurt and betrayed, since the further they get from the Marshall Plan and the closer they get to Star Wars, the more grudging is Euro-admiration.

BRIT-THINK: Brits feel that patriotism (other people's) is cheap emotion. The last refuge of a scoundrel. Vulgar, and intellectually third-rate. All of which makes them proud to be British.

Brits manage, they feel, a better class of patriotism. It is restrained and formalized ritual, which only *hints* at the swelling breast beneath. A demonstration of natural superiority in judgement, taste and style ... high-quality stuff. God is an Englishman.

In truth, they conduct celebrations of self-love in much the same way as Yanks. There's not a great deal of distance between the red, white and blue parachutes at a half-time display, and the changing of the guard outside Buckingham Palace. Few rituals can be as extravagant as a royal wedding, complete with horse-drawn coaches, fanfare of trumpets and diamonds glinting in the sun. But Brits are convinced that such pomp and circumstance is somehow 'different' — allowable. Stately rather than self-indulgent. Anyway: 'we do it so well!' There is something fundamentally tasteful about dressing your Queen in riding clothes, and making her perch side-saddle on a skittish horse reviewing her troops for hours. In the rain. On her birthday.

Eco-chauvinism

AMERI-SPEND: In the same way as Ameri-patriotism is wrapped up with Hollywood, it merges too with Madison Avenue. To make a purchase, in America, is a patriotic gesture. Goods are confused with greatness. 'Plotkin Chevrolet,' a local TV ad will enjoin. 'We *are* America!' No Brit-product will make a similarly grandiose claim. The most you can expect is 'Go to work on a British egg.' Or 'Cheddar cheese . . . a taste of Britain.'

Buy British:

BRIT-THINK: As citizens of a trading nation, Brits are always concerned with trade deficits. Periodically, they fight back — at the Japanese, or the Americans, or the rest of the EEC — by launching a 'Buy British' campaign. This is often carried to ridiculous extremes of Gross National Patriotism. There are heated arguments about how British milk tastes better than the inferior French variety, why British margarine is preferable to imported Aussie brands, and how Brit-bacon makes better Brit-breakfasts than popular Danish imports. Brits can become positively xenophobic when the dominance of domestic meat, or leather goods, or coal (hotter heat, quarried by British workers) is under threat. Yanks, by contrast, rarely seem to notice what's American and what isn't, and generally assume that (electrical goods, cars and South African apples apart) everything *is*. Which is why they are presently carrying the world's largest trade deficit. Bob Hope's doing his best to heighten awareness by appearing in TV commercials sporting sports jackets labelled, 'Made In The USA — It Matters' . . . but to little avail. Ameri-patriotism does not seem to manifest itself in fierce allegiance to polyester fibre and slices of bacon.

Dollar allegiance . . . big bucks

AMERI-THINK: To Yanks, the only spectacle as moving as the Stars and Stripes flying over a baseball stadium (or a Chevy dealership) is the reassuring sight

84

and crunch of a crisp greenback. Though many Americans these days are widely travelled, dollar-dependency is a hard habit to break. They do not trust anyone else's money, and (stuff the foreign exchange-rates) have never been convinced that any currency in the world is worth more than the almighty buck. Or indeed is worth anything at all.

They're also convinced that if only Brits (and others) had the choice, they'd rather deal in dollars than the local stuff anyday. The point is that no one plays around with bucks. Solid as rocks. They never slide dramatically, even when trade deficits are huge. They're never 'devalued', whatever that means. No one makes them into tinny little gold coins that look like they have chocolate inside. Other countries have financial crises because they can't get their acts together; reliable countries have well-behaved money. A country gets the currency it deserves.

Currencies for which Yanks have some respect (in descending order):

1 the Swiss franc
2 the West German mark
3 the yen
4 the pound
5 the French franc (only just)
6 anything Scandinavian (but not *Finnish*, which is different)
7 the South African krugerrand
8 the Italian lira (this is really pushing it)

> NOTE* Aussie and Canadian dollars are virtually 'proxy' currencies, pegged to the UK pound and the US dollar respectively.

But this is a choice of evils. It's generally unwise to trade perfectly good greenbacks for something which is bound to be inferior. When travelling, keep your fist full of dollars, and if they won't take them, use AMEX.

Pound of flesh

BRIT-THINK: How are the mighty fallen! The pound is permanently pegged in Brit-minds at $3 or so (the old guinea) when the average Brit earned around ten of them a week. There was no such thing as inflation or currency fluctuation, and the world was a far better place.

It is a cliché to say so, but the concept of *one pound sterling* still has for Brits a physical reality; visions of bags of silver, enough to satisfy Nelson Bunker-Hunt. They cannot rid themselves of the notion that a pound is a lot of money, and that OAPs should be able to live comfortably on three or four of them a week. Successive Brit-governments have saved huge sums by perpetuating this eco-anachronism, with the result that most elderly people now suffer real hardship, 20,000 leagues beneath the poverty-line. Today's pound will scarcely buy a round-trip tube fare across central London, but Brit-minds and Brit-flation are wildly out of sync.

This explains an aspect of behaviour which often appears odd to Yanks . . . a Brit's compulsion to preserve every coin as if it were his last, and to insist that Yank tourists do the same.

You're a stranger here dear? You dont want to take this bus to Knightsbridge - not from Oxford Circus - it's very dear, dear - cost you 60p. Take the 27 to Marble Arch, change again for an 11 heading towards Shepherds Bush, get off at Lancaster Gate, walk through the Park to Kensington, then get a 52 to Knightsbridge. You'll save twenty pence.

There is still immense pride in the pound, of course. For a start, it has a picture of the Queen on it. Second, it is measured in sensible ones or twos or fives, and you do not require 10,000 of it to buy a lamb chop, like *some* currencies Brits could mention. Finally, notes are paper promises to 'pay the bearer on demand the sum of X'; and everyone knows that a Brit's word is his bond. Especially if you have it in writing.

Time was when Brits would accept no other currency. Today, there are lots of things they'd rather have than pounds. These are, in descending order:

1 Mega-bucks
2 Big bucks
3 Bucks
 ... plus a handful of Brit-change
 to put in parking meters.

13 What makes this country great?

The very, very best things in America

1 A telephone system which *works*, and has:
   (a) the same number of digits whether you're dialing Philly or Fresno, and
   (b) operators who seem to know *all* the letters in the alphabet.
2 Electrical goods sold complete with plugs, which will run off any outlet in the country. Standardized 'screw-in' lightbulbs to take the guesswork out of shopping.
3 Discount drugstores (open 24 hours).
4 Watchable breakfast TV.
5 The only drinkable skimmed milk in the world.
6 The world's best ice cream (sorry, Italians).
7 The world's best cheesecake (sorry, Germans).
8 Automatic ice-water on restaurant tables.
9 Fahrenheit temperatures, inches, feet and yards.

The best of British

1 A postal system which *works*. Most first-class letters arrive within 24 hours of posting. Delays of more than 48 hours are taken as evidence of social breakdown, and the Government offers to resign.
2 Understanding of the restorative value of tea with milk at teatime.
3 London's black cabs. Clean, plenty of headroom, all doors convincingly attached, and drivers who know the way.
4 Wake-up alarm calls which can be booked.
5 World's cleverest shop-window displays.
6 World's best and most stylish TV commercials.
7 Milk delivered daily to the doorstep.
8 Doctors who still make house-calls (off-set by chemists who won't open at night or on weekends so you can fill the prescription).
9 World's grooviest and most inventive hairdressers (pink highlights, madame?).

The very, very best things in America

10 Hospital buildings which do not increase the mortality rate by *depressing* patients to death.
11 A healthy number of medical malpractice suits, which keep doctors on their toes.
12 Washcloths in hotel bedrooms.
13 Ted Koppel, the world's best television interviewer.
14 Zillions of places where you can get it wholesale ... whatever it is.
15 Shops and department stores which take returns without moving on to a war footing.
16 Best, cheapest and most competitive domestic airline system in the world.
17 World's most entertaining political campaigns (money no object).
18 The existence of genuine summer.
19 Grocery shopping-bags made of tough, strong paper. Supermarket packers who fill them for you, then carry them to your car.
20 Bathrooms with shower-power. (Brit shower-heads are for decorative purposes only.)
21 Unleaded gas (for sale at popular prices).
22 *Hot* toast for breakfast (no toast-racks) and unlimited refills on coffee.
23 Intuitive understanding of how to treat a hamburger.

The best of British

10 Upholstered seats in London tubes.
11 Best Italian restaurants of any city in the world, including Rome.
12 Best Indian restaurants of any city in the world, including Delhi.
13 Some of the world's best theatres, and tickets which are still cheap(ish).
14 Great bookstores, cut-price paperbacks.
15 City streets which are safe(ish).
16 The survival of the traditional British nanny (which has ensured the survival of the 2-career family).
17 The only significant gay population not yet decimated by AIDS.
18 Police who, as a rule, do not carry guns, and have lots of friends who help them with their inquiries.
19 High interest-rates on ordinary deposit accounts.
20 Real town-houses in the centres of big cities, some still in single-family occupation.
21 Truly prurient gossip-columns appearing daily in respectable national newspapers.
22 National newspapers.
23 Public transport systems that do.

The very, very best things in America

24 Giant, frost-free refrigerators with ice-cube dispensers on the outside.

25 Central heating systems that mean business.

26 Waitresses who take an interest, and will really discuss with you whether you're going to enjoy the blintzes more with sour cream or cinnamon.

27 Sports events still attended by 'families', and people who have not done time for G.B.H.

28 The ability to mix a good cocktail (this is unique on the planet).

The best of British

24 Preference for real wool carpet (100%) at prices which stop just short of ludicrous.

25 Wonderful parks, where civic authorities indulge the public fascination for plant-life.

26 World's most beautiful traditional 'prams'. Won't fold away and store in cars, but perfect for wheeling baby-Brits through world's most beautiful parks.

27 Appreciation of cream. Cream cakes, clotted cream teas, coffee with real cream, strawbs with cream at Wimbledon. Liquid double cream poured liberally over your already obscenely fattening fudge cake.

28 Harrods and Harvey Nichols (where most British women would like to be forced to remain under house-arrest).

14 Sex

Differences between Anglo- and Ameri-sex are mostly *oral*. Which is to say that Yanks talk more *about* it, then talk more while *doing* it, since sex in America is the stuff of endless self-examination. Brits are somewhat less introspective about sex, though the gap has been narrowing since the Sixties. In general, they like to 'get on with it', while Yanks experience full erotic catharsis only if they've talked it through first.

The main thing that British men will notice about American women is how much they talk. The average Yankette will probably utter 30%–50% more words in a lifetime than her UK counterpart. It takes this much verbiage to tell people about herself ('lay herself entirely open') and to broadly explain her expectations (so that the 'relationship' can begin on a sound footing, the possibilities of misunderstanding minimized).

To summarize 20 years' worth or so of speech — she doesn't want a lot: merely to be blissfully happy, extravagantly rich, acclaimed for her achievements and personal style, idolized by her husband and children, publicly perceived as divinely beautiful, and on first-name terms with the President. And she wants her partner/husband to make it all happen ('Having It All') while at the same time providing regular and euphoric sex.

Ameri-male knows where his duty lies. He's read the books and magazines which say she needs to feel independent and capable, yet needed and passionately desired. He's not stupid. It's been a long time since the Sixties, when he painfully learned new 'responses' toward women, and purged traces of revisionist M.C.P. thought. Now, he's a New Man; eyes open, consciousness raised. We're talking *earnest*, here. Yes, for Yuppie Man (and influential Baby-Boomers) at least, years of feminist agitation (words again) have at last begun to change *attitudes*. What was hip affectation, mere lip service to women, has gone deep throat. Pay-off time. We've entered the First Age of Post-Tokenist America.

This does *not* mean that women have finally caught up with men in terms of money, power and job opportunity. (It's often presented as significant that women control one-third of all the wealth in America ... but most of them are widows.) What it *does* mean — to the sharp observer — are small but significant changes in male behaviour.

Take any Yuppie dinner party. *Who* dominates the conversation over the cold-vegetable-pate-with-fresh-tomato-and-basil-sauce? No, *not* the Gary Hart look-alikes reviewing the day's vicissitudes on Wall Street. They are strangely silent, solicitous and attentive while the *women* de-brief. They do not compete, they listen hard, paying the undivided attention which Brit-woman reserves, in similar circumstances, for Brit-Man. In Post-tokenist America, women expect to *steer* the conversation ... not merely to punctuate it with occasional girlish giggles.

Every so often the New American Man will interject. Nothing Macho about sport or finance calculated to seize control and exclude the female company. Instead, he opens with something about urban interior design, or educational theory. He may ask to see pictures of other guests' children (and he won't be gauche enough to assume that only the *mother* carries them.) Then he may offer to show some of his own.

BRIT-THINK: Brit-woman has (anti-sex discrimination laws notwithstanding) scarcely made it to the Tokenist — let alone Post-Tokenist — Age. Years of pro-feminist conditioning have not really cut across the set of rigid social and sexual boundaries fixed in the minds of Brit-males. In spite of herself (and her raised consciousness), Ms Brit spends a lot of time being grateful to men for small favours. She reacts this way to bosses, sons and lovers. She shares her mother's conviction that you can get what you want without confrontation; by applying a little 'female psychology', and 'humouring him'. Let him think it's his idea.

In this way, Brit-woman dooms herself to a life of good-natured helplessness. She has no real power-base, and lacks the courage to take the spotlight and stand her ground. She is apologetic about raising the subjects which interest her most, and — in mixed groups — covers them fleetingly, badly, assuming that she is boring the men present. She feels presumptuous when required to engage a husband's attention on a 'feminine' issue ... the choice of wallpaper, for example, or her approaching hysterectomy ... thus dragging him from more pressing male concerns (the fortunes of Manchester United).

Progress at work is slow-to-non-existent. Brit-male cannot bring himself to repose real confidence in her, and sees her rather as the monkey riding the bicycle. He does not expect her to do it well; the wonder is that she does it at all. Even when he likes her, and recognizes her abilities and achievements, he is unlikely to push for her promotion. (Brits like good things to stay *as they are*.) Furthermore, he cannot see her as a serious answer to corporate problems. If she shows any inclination to hustle, or force his hand — if, for one moment, she betrays her ambition — she will lose his goodwill. He will automatically obstruct her. He doesn't know why; but he can't help himself.

In Britain, only *women* have read the right magazines (or articles on 'women's pages' in newspapers) since real men have better things to do with their time. Brit-woman is primed to expect a shift in attitudes, a new form of 'sexual contract' along American lines ... and she's prepared to keep her side of the bargain. (Problem is, she's the only one who *knows* there's a bargain.) So she's motivated to become a better and more interesting person, to dress well, diet, keep fit, and otherwise hold back the ravages of time. *He* does not always return the compliment, preferring to sit carpet-slippered in his favourite arm-chair and/or oldest jeans, eyes fixed firmly on the telly, fist clenching a can of something, teeth in desperate need of smokers' tooth-polish. He is, he's convinced, a prize. 'After all, I'm *here*, aren't I?' What he means is that she's lucky he's at home filling the armchair, when he could be out boring some other nice girl to death.

Marriage of true minds:
Anglo-Ameri-matrimony

The thing that strikes a Yank most forcibly on overhearing a conversation between a British husband-and-wife in a restaurant, or on a train, is that they carry on as if they've never met each other before.

What, Yanks wonder, have they been *talking* about for the past twenty years? They themselves (because they talk so much) have long ago exhausted most conversational generalities, and worked down to the gory details.

The point is that Brits are great respecters of each others' privacy (which is another way of saying that they don't communicate much). They are careful not to 'intrude', even in close family situations. This is evident in relationships between parents and children, where grown-ups believe in 'butting out' and letting little Oliver or Fiona make their own mistakes. Brit-parents are frequently seen to stand back while the sprogs head straight for the precipice; putting a brave face on things and cheerfully skating over the formalities of conversation.

Gimme Space...

Yanks, on the other hand, close in on each other. They consider that intimacy confers a kind of emotional Carte Blanche, and use it without reservation to save their nearest and dearest from themselves. They worry away at their 'relationships', examining, probing. Every psyche is up for grabs. Being in love means never having to back off.

So, there's lots of gratuitous comment on each other's 'hang-ups' and 'real motivations'. Americans are the world's greatest psycho-nags. Cruel — and amateur — dissections are commonplace.

Brits and Yanks in love

Brit-male resists falling in love in the first place by adopting an attitude towards women which is ... dismissive. He often casts them as 'joke' figures, which relieves him of any need to treat them seriously. The precise way in which this is done varies from region-to-region; but a short acquaintance with TV comedy reveals that:

1 In the South

   She is often portrayed as brainless and over-sexed. After he nails her, he can't remember her name. Nor she his.

2 In the North

   Sex is, for him, a purely passive affair, in which she is the voracious predator. He runs for his life from her unsolicited attentions, much preferring a game of snooker with the lads. For her part, when she is not running salivating after him, she is bending iron bars with her bare hands.

What with one thing and another, it is easy to form the impression that Brit-male does not really like women much. This is not true. He does, in fact, desire them passionately, and is inclined to pursue them, as long as he does not have to talk to them too.

American women generally find British men attractive and sexy, and are often prepared to marry them — i.e., Linda and Paul McCartney, Chrissie Evert and John Lloyd, Wallis Simpson and King Edward VIII, Caroline and Tony Wedgewood Benn, and Winston Churchill's mum and dad. With rare exceptions, this is a mistake, since America is something of a matriarchy, while Britain (Mrs T. notwithstanding) is not. If Yankette simply does what comes naturally, every lover's tiff will bring with it the charge that she is 'pushy' and 'aggressive' . . . or just plain loud.

Of course, there are romantic compensations. He 'speaks so beautifully' (when he speaks). An English accent sounds far more seductive than the casual Yank-approach: 'Hiya, kid, wanna dance?' He uses expressions she's never heard on the lips of a man, like 'oh, lovely' . . . causing her to wonder if he is sensitive and passionate, or just gay. (Real Ameri-men don't eat quiche or say 'oh, lovely'.)

His relative diffidence presents problems; a lack of willingness on his part to join her in analysing the relationship. This comes as something of a shock. Ameri-bride knows Brits to be an articulate people, skilled at public debate. But they seem to reserve their best stuff for perfect strangers, or formal speaking engagements, or the West End stage, or the floor of the House of Commons, or the telly. They don't waste much energy at home. After the first flush of a new relationship, love-talk dries. Brits quickly run out of steam and enthusiasm for examination and appraisal. (No conversational staying-power.) In fact, once married, they see no further *need* for conversation. This is why it takes them ten to fifteen years to find out how their partners like coffee.

Serious sex

AMERI-THINK: Yanks Treat Sex Seriously (as they do all other areas of personal development). They approach it with the earnestness and single-minded determination you'd expect from a marathon runner in training. They mean to win, to experience the Ultimate Orgasm. And they like to do things scientifically.

God helps those who help themselves. As a college undergrad, Ameri-male has read all the right books, can reel off 82 erotic pressure-points, 30 'most successful' positions, 16 sure-fire manual techniques and the location of the 'G'-spot. Like all Americans, he reposes great confidence in 'expertise' (anything which is written down) and is concerned to achieve his own — and his partner's — full erotic potential. He is not a great lover, but he is *committed*. Someday, it may all come naturally, but not yet. He doesn't trust his own instincts, and it's a bit . . . deliberate. All his foreplay comes from p.25 of the *Superstud's Handbook*.

BRIT-IN-BED: Nothing so testing for Super-Brit, who wouldn't dream of brushing up on technique; 'something you're born with, or forget it'. He prides himself on being instinctive in bed, which is not necessarily the same as 'generous'. To be fair, it is between the sheets that he seems to shine; to magically shed the plethora of inhibitions which dog the rest of his waking life. He becomes rather creative, certainly catholic in his tastes and even *experimental*. A Brit experimental is a Brit abandoned.

Post-coitally . . .

Ameri-man will remain physically close to his partner, because it says in the book how much she hates it when men roll away and snore. Drained and exhausted, he turns mentally to page 26, and continues to demonstrate tenderness.

Super-Brit has no such reservations, reverting instantly to type . . . and usually to silence. If he knows the line, he muffs it. Instead of 'I love you and I enjoyed it', he mutters something about 'enjoying you and loving it'.

Choosing a partner

The same lack of confidence which encourages Yanks to 'go by the book' in matters sexual extends to other areas. Trickiest of all is *Choosing A Partner*. This is because there's no guide to refer to; no book on the market called *Is She A Dog?* or *Are You Shacked Up With A Turkey?*. Yanks hate to chance an independent decision, terrified that their selections will fail to measure up. This explains why the US has led the way in designer labels on everything from jeans to track-shoes, and pillowcases to perfumes. If you've no confidence in your own taste, you can purchase someone else's.

In the same way, Yanks will look for romantic partners who carry some form of endorsement. Ambitious Ameri-male demands a designer-label girl. Christie Brinkley — the fabled Uptown Girl — is a fine

98

example. Someone famous who is the child of someone famous has rare endorsement. Ditto an actress (*other* people admire her and pay to see her), an ex-wife or girl-friend of someone famous (she's already been singled out for the Big Time) — or simply a girl who owns a mink. If someone else bought it, he liked her a lot. If she bought it for herself, her boss thought enough of her to pay her a high salary. Either way, Ameri-male is on safe, well-trodden turf, and can relax.

Ms America is just as quick to seek hallmarks of quality. For her, it's not so much a question of who had him first, as where he's *been*. For instance, to Harvard or Yale or somewhere in the Ivy League for a post-graduate degree. Does his employer like him — is he in line for a junior partnership in his law firm? Does he come with matching, upwardly-mobile friends? Are his own accoutrements (his Brooks Brothers suits, his Mercedes Sports Coupé, his choice of health-club and apartment) Yup-to-the-minute? Does he like himself? Does his shrink like him? If so, he's worth a try.

Once partner-choice is legitimized by marriage, Yank arrivistes continue to be influenced by endorsements and recognized seals of approval. As part of the tough climb to the top, they will periodically bestow on each other certain symbols of success. Each one reminds the world that they have, in choosing each other, chosen well.

She gets:

1 Her fur. A blackglama mink, natural fitch, coyote, silver fox or even lynx if she insists.
2 Her Mercedes (sport)
3 A new diamond solitaire to replace her original engagement ring. Pear-shaped, and 3.5 carats *at least*.
4 Authentic Cartier tank wrist-watch to replace Seiko copy. A gold and diamond Piaget for evening.
5 A piece of Real Art to hang in the apartment. She likes Matisse and Miro, and Hockney and Warhol prints.
6 A face-lift (after she's consulted surgeons in different parts of America).
7 A week at a health-club in Palm Springs to recuperate.
8 Her trip to Europe, with a week at the Byblos in St Tropez.

He gets:

1 A camel-coloured cashmere overcoat, and a Bijan suit which makes him feel fat.
2 His Mercedes
3 A brown alligator briefcase with computer-locking device.
4 A portable car 'phone which fits into the briefcase and hooks on to his golf-cart.
5 A selection of Gucci loafers (which hurt).
6 His office re-decorated in post-modernist minimalist, which means rag-rolled walls and nowhere to sit.
7 His eyelids done and a hair transplant in front (her surgeon was a genius).
8 Her trip to Europe. (He'd rather be on the golf-course.)

They get:

9 A condo in Florida (he wants one on a golf-course, she argues for something in Boca with an ocean view).
10 A personal 'trainer' who visits the house twice a week to lead them in a custom-designed exercise programme ... 'otherwise, we're so undisciplined!'

... with such offerings do Ameri-husbands and wives mark success, and worship at the shrine of their own marriage.

Specific gifts are less important to the Brit-couple, whose sense of belonging stems from a mutual understanding of birthright. (Outward signs of Getting There and Being There are not so crucial when you're Born There.) And, Brits needn't be well-born to feel secure. The unshakeable sense of identity comes from knowing — and accepting —your place in the social order. It's one of the reasons the class-system survives. And Britain threatens not to.

Anyway, Brit-male does not see his wife as living testimony to his achievements. This takes the pressure off her, but also means that he doesn't much interest himself in the way she looks. If she is middle-aged, she is too often a drab. He doesn't seem to notice (and she has ceased to care) that her roots are grey, her winter coat too short and out of style, her old banger of a car rusting at the bottom and falling apart. He *does* notice that there's a bald patch forming in the garden lawn. Over in the far corner.

Which is *not* to say that Brit-success has no material trappings. Here are a few.

Arrivistes get:

1 A bigger garden for a bigger splash. Possibly a pool, a state-of-the-art power mower for that striped effect. Expensive herbaceous borders and stonework ornaments of pre-cast concrete. A wrought-iron gazebo which they call 'the summer house'.

2 House in the country (possibly attached to the garden). Georgian or Regency for preference, Victorian at a pinch. If it's got original Tudor or Elizabethan bits attached, Brits are ecstatic.

3 Horses and people to take care of the horses and friends to admire the estate and ride the horses.

4 A Range-Rover to transport the friends who ride the horses.

She gets:

1 Invited to a Royal garden party.
2 A live-in nanny.
3 'Real' antique furniture made of English oak or mahogany ... (nothing 'repro').
4 Hand-painted nursery furniture for the children's rooms ('so *sweet* with Arabella's name on her little dressing-table').
5 A genuine Aga cast-iron stove, enameled to match the farmhouse kitchen by Smallbone of Devizes.
6 Dogs — preferably large, slavering and pedigreed —to splodge around on quarry-tiled floors.
7 Silk head-scarves printed with horsey themes for wearing outdoors and reminding one of the Royal Family; lengths of wool tartan or black velvet to make floor-length evening skirts for dinner parties 'at home'.
8 A yearly subscription to *Tatler* and *Country Life*.
9 A winter ski holiday somewhere French or Swiss. Nanny comes too, to keep the children happy on the nursery slopes ... 'she's doing frightfully well!'
10 Summer hols in Cap Ferrat (at the home of friends).
11 The most expensive personalized Christmas cards she can find at Fortnum's.

He Gets:

1 His name on the New Year's Honours List.
2 To fantasize about the chance of a future knighthood.
3 New status as a Civic Leader, by buying the local football club.
(He puts *her* name on one of the stands.)
4 Flattering solicitations for funds from: the local art gallery/repertory company/hospital/church/newspaper
5 Photographed and interviewed a great deal by the local newspaper.
6 A new accountant, and
7 A desire to leave the country for tax reasons.

They Get:

1 Headaches, worrying whether to let nanny drive the XJS.

15 The children . . .
Baby-Brit, Baby-Yank

AMERI-THINK: The whole purpose of Having It All is passing It All on to your children. No matter how humble your own origins, It All is your child's birthright. Remember that America is the Land of Opportunity where any kid can grow up to be President, even if her name is Lisa.

Today's Ameri-parents feel compelled to help a child get the jump on others. Gone are the days when you could sit back, and let him develop at his own pace. The 1980s are all about the survival of the fittest; and a parent's highest duty is to position pride-and-joy for success. Ameri-kids in the fast track need to progress:

1 from neo-natal sensory training to
2 the best Montessori pre-school, to
3 early Kindergarten entrance, and
4 the city's top-rated elementary school with 'advanced ability' classes or a 'gifted' programme, to
5 the most competitive junior high and high school, with the vital run-up to S.A.T.s and possible early admission to
6 an Ivy League University with a first-rate reputation in pre-law, plus a grueling one-year crammer to prepare for crucial L.S.A.Ts and
7 America's finest law schools, where a respectable performance leads at last to
8 partnership in prestige law firm charging wildly exorbitant fees, and guaranteeing for progeny and progenitors

. . . a piece of the AMERICAN DREAM.

The fiercer the competition, the more determined is Ameri-parent. He will not let himself off the hook. If all things are possible, there is no reason for failure, apart from poor planning. At each step along the way his task is to help his infant jockey for a front position in the fray.

Call yourself a parent when your kid never: studied Suzuki violin/swam before he walked/read before he swam? Can you walk tall if he's not computer-literate at 8? Who's his private baseball/gymnastics coach? Is he enrolled at summer tennis camp? Has he seen a nutritionist/does anyone speak to him in Spanish/when does he get hidden braces on his teeth?

Yank parents seldom hold with the sentimental notion of loving and accepting a child simply for what he is. They love him, alright, but they're happy to try and improve upon nature. If he needs help, he needs help. His destiny is in their hands.

So, they set themselves the rather schizoid task of boosting the child's self-esteem ('Eric, you are a wonderful and worthwhile person . . . a winner!') while at the same time remaining detached enough to take an objective view. If Eric is stuck with a big nose, crooked teeth, a dud personality and trouble with long division, all-American parents will fix it. They are the only parents in the world with the inclination and the resources to re-assemble their kids if they don't like them.

No effort is too great. Enormous amounts of time, energy and money are expended on Ameri-kid in the fond hope that, someday, even the least promising specimen will turn up trumps. He'll be a credit to his parents; President, perhaps, or better still — rich. Interestingly, however much time he spends being hot-housed to perfection, he spends still more engaged in one vital and patriotic activity. GOING OUT TO DINNER. Yes, Ameri-parents take their children everywhere, since junior is entitled to the best, and 'the best' is defined by what his parents do. They like to 'expose' him to everything (diseases apart). He is the focus of all their attention, and they are inordinately proud of him . . . even if he's at a relatively primitive stage of development. They're constantly torn between conflicting desires to compliment him, and nag him to death. They compromise by doing both; and taking an obsessive interest in every fibre of his (by now ample) being.

Ameri-parents characteristically probe the infant psyche as they do each other's in romance, examining, analysing, discussing. He has no place to hide. He is their Great White Hope, and they reserve the right to drive him crazy while worshipping at the shrine.

BRIT-THINK: Brit-parents take a child more or less as he comes. If he comes with crooked teeth, they'll stay crooked. A weak chin will continue to recede. Not for them a survey of plastic surgeons, gathering opinions on whether to pin back his ears. Unless there's a medical imperative, Brits

You coughed Eric, I heard you cough Muriel I'm taking him to the Mayo clinic its ridiculous he coughs once maybe twice a week - look Eric I know you didn't do all that well at beginning French but we want you to know its ok we can have you coached its not the end of the world you're a terrific kid really terrific smart too if it doesn't pick up by next semester we'll try a specialist school in Boston get your hands out of those potato chips you want to get high cholesterol...

(including affluent ones) dislike interfering with nature. They will refine his natural attributes in two areas only:

1 His accent. This will concern them, as it must be *at least* as good as theirs, and if possible, better. If he fails to pass muster in this important respect, he is socially doomed ... separated from his parents by the Brit-system of aural segregation. Stressful years are spent trying to counteract the influence of his scruffy friends, who can't complete a full sentence without a glottal stop ... ''ullo, Mrs, c'n oi 'ave a bo'ull of soda?'

2 His table manners. These can truly affect his life. At the first opportunity his tiny fist is unclenched from the fork he wields like an ice-pick. His earliest words are, 'please-may-I-get-down?' By the time he is 8, he's taught to understand the proper use of a fish knife. If his table manners are impeccable, the logic goes, no one will notice his teeth.

Brit-parent is, like his American counterpart, enormously proud of his offspring. But, for reasons he can't explain, he'd rather die than express it. There's a lot of good-natured banter about how hopeless little Jeremy is, usually conducted outside the child's earshot, with adult friends who can be counted upon to be just as disparaging about their own kids.

This is a Brit-ritual which should not be taken at face-value. Parents merely *pretend* to be detached, resigned and objective so that real feelings are disguised; it's bad form to score points off another child, or to show off. In truth, they think that small Jeremy is bloody marvellous. Big ears and all.

The disparagement will continue — to a lesser extent — in front of the child him/herself. Not for Brit-kid the continually massaged ego of his American counterpart. Too much praise is not *good* for him. It will make him pig-headed and insufferable. Worse still, it may make him *precocious* (despised in a Brit-child, but much valued by American

106

parents, who feel it's important to be *forward*). Brit-parents still consider that modesty and humility are virtues. Americans see them as self-imposed handicaps.

Spending time with the kids

Ameri-parents are so publicly proud of their children (even while they're still at the awkward, prototype stage) that they:

1   want to be near them all the time (i.e., in restaurants)
2   talk about them at the slightest encouragement (so certain are they that the finished product will be a knock-out)
3   assume that everyone else is smitten, and would like to spend time with them, too.

So, a word of warning: if British adults meet Americans on holiday (when it can be seen or assumed that the Yanks have brought young Eric along) Brits should be wary of making dinner arrangements unless they crave his company as well. Yanks openly admire their children, and wish to share them. They assume that you — a friend — will actually *want* to meet their relatives/kids/families ... whereas Brits make the reasonable assumption that nothing could be further from your thoughts.

Brit parents do not by habit call attention to their children until they are young adults, and relatively presentable (capable of using a fish knife with confidence). The affluent upper (and upper middle) classes have for years operated a system of infant Apartheid, under which children are treated as separate, and unequal. In prosperous families they are kept under wraps for years, relegated to nannies and boarding-schools. Years ago, Victorian parents did not formally meet their children until they'd reached 17.

The legacy of this system remains in many households. Children from up-market families seldom eat an evening meal with their parents; at 5 p.m. or so, they take nursery tea with nanny. This is a traditional collation of stodge-on-starch (bread-and-butter with biscuits and cakes) devised in days when no one understood the connection between protein and growth. The practice survives because this is Britain, and 'we've always done it this way'. Anyway, Brit-parents seem to consider that children are only small, and do not need to eat like real people.

Such children also wear short pants in December, because 'they don't feel the cold'. No one knows if they experience pain. This is why Brits maintain corporal punishment in schools, and feel there is an argument for walloping people too little to fight back. (Brits pride themselves on being a civilized lot, and one of the only nations in the world too humane to beat convicted criminals. They do it to their children instead.)

They also scrimp and sacrifice to send them to boarding-schools of Draconian comfortlessness, which they attended themselves, and which ruined their own childhoods. They do this because 'One Does', and because it 'develops character' (not to mention head-lice). Most important, it Teaches One How To Behave. In short, it encourages impressionable kiddie-clone to imitate the mannerisms of everyone else at boarding-school, so that he can for evermore recognize and be recognized by members of his own social set. He is now equipped with *British Radar*. Entrée into his exclusive club is the Anglo-version of designer labelling.

What's in a nickname?

Brits take names Very Seriously. They treat their own with great respect (since they are part of proud traditions of class and family) and resist shortening them. Yanks — who can rarely trace their ancestors or their names back further than Ellis Island — are more casual. Anyway — how protective can you be about Yablonsky or Lipschitz?

Everyone knows that Americans use names in conversation far more than the British do. When a Yank is introduced to you for the first time, he'll have a contest with himself to see how many times he can repeat your handle in a sentence. Names appeal to an American's sense of the importance of the individual ... and he prefers first names to last ones. Using yours a lot is his way of getting friendly. He means it as a compliment — and each usage is testimony to your uniqueness as a human being. In Ameri-culture, over-use of a first name indicates that someone is paying attention to you. If it sounds ingratiating, it is also flattering.

Brits avoid using names if at all possible. To address relative strangers so directly strikes them as presumptuous ... something of a liberty.

They prefer to preserve a bit of distance. So, the higher your social status, the lower the likelihood of being called by name. Other Brits — as a courtesy and mark of respect — will simply pretend that you don't have one. Instead, they'll substitute official titles ('Hello, Chairman', or 'yes, Minister') or fall back on the anonymous 'certainly, Madame'. Unlike Yanks, they will avoid referring to anyone as 'Sir' unless he is a Peer of the Realm. Americans throw the term around, since it's no indication of rank. They call *everyone* 'Sir' if they:

1 want to sell him something, or
2 mean to be nice, and
3 didn't catch his first name.

Furthermore, Americans like and cultivate nicknames, even when they are grown men at the top of the corporate or political tree. They do not feel demeaned by diminutives, or 'cute' handles: (see 'Cute', p. 67). How else do you explain 'Ronnie' Reagan, or 'Jimmy' Carter, 'Tip' O'Neill, 'Bebe' Rebozo or 'Swifty' Lazarre?

The truth is that nicknames make Americans feel *liked* — especially if they have an 'ee' sound on the end: Judy, Janie, Dickie, Billy, Katie, Dougie, Wendy, Normie. Given the chance, they will tack an 'ee' on to the unlikeliest names; if an English friend is called Nigel, he becomes 'Nigey'. If the proper name *already* contains an 'ee' sound (i.e., Sidney)

Yanks will re-arrange it, so that it ends in an even more affectionate 'ee'. For example, 'Sidley'. If you don't acquire an 'ee' on the end of your name soon after Americans meet you, chances are that they don't like you much.

Yanks also enjoy choosing fairly brutal and insulting nicknames for male friends ... particularly if these are shortened versions of unpronounceable Middle European surnames. Slobovoditch goes through life as 'slob', Yablonsky as 'yob', Buitoni as 'boo boo' and Spitalney as 'spit'. These are carried with pride, and often endure well into adult life.

The Brit version is a somewhat gentler affair, and usually a play on the last name, since parents are at pains to give first names which 'can't be shortened'. Every time they speak to little Nigel, or Olympia or Tarquin, or call them to tea, they repeat the whole impressive handle. No Nige, or Ollie, or Tark. Mini-Brits are encouraged to take themselves rather seriously in this respect.

As soon as they leave the house, the whole thing is up for grabs. Super-Brit surnames are specially at risk, and quickly reduced. 'Faversham' becomes 'Favvers', 'Bothrington' equals 'Bothers'. If you're at boarding-school, and unfortunate enough to be part of a family of boys called 'Ramsbottom', it's Bottoms maximus and minimus. In the best circles, America's favourite ethnic nicknames are right out. It's safe to say that virtually no one at Eton or Gordonstown gets called 'Bubulah'.

Finally: it is a scientifically documentable fact that the *shorter* an adult male Brit is, the less likely he is to let you abbreviate his name. Forcing you to repeat eighteen syllables seems to increase his sense of stature. Just try calling Jonathan Frederick Hethrington-Spiers 'Johnie' — or 'Jon Jon' — and see how he likes it.

What's in a name

Yanks are never, ever called:

Nigel, Neville, Arabella, Tarquin, Sian, Fionna, Pippa, Dermot, Derek, Trevor, Gemma, Giles, Morag, Clyde, Coriander, Olympia, Nichola, Briony, Sebastian, Bronwyn, Candida, Philippa, Lavinia, Miranda, Tristram

In America, these are girls' names:

Robin, Jamie, Adrienne, Laurie, Leslie

Brits are never, ever called:

Murray, Seymour, Irv, Mitzi, Farrah, Ashley, Herb, Sheldon, Cuthbert, Billie-Jo, Adelaide, Ralph, Merv, Mindy, Candy, Sissy, Brooke, Shannon, Babe, Marcy, Melissa, Dwight, Duane, Buddy, Rock, Ridge, Tab.

In Britain, these are boys' names:

Robin, Jaime, Adrian, Laurie, Leslie

The American nickname you can't have in Britain:

Randy. To Brits, it does not sound like a diminutive of Randolph. It is a bit like going around calling yourself 'sex-crazed'.

16 The golden years . . . Life begins at 60

Giving in gracefully . . .

BRIT-THINK: People should not try too hard to hold back the ravages of time. Face-lifts and jogging geriatrics are vaguely obscene. One should grow old gracefully, bow to the inevitable . . . (be content to look dreadful). It's ghastly and unnatural to throw it about like Joan Collins. All older women (anyone past 50) should chose as a role-model for dress and decorum the Queen Mum. The Queen certainly has.

Any Brit over 65, regardless of financial circumstances, rejoices in the title of 'old-age pensioner' — abbreviated to OAP. The label is designed to depress him to death quickly, thus saving money for the State. In order to help speed the elderly on their way, Brits have devised a *State Pension Scheme* which gives a whole new meaning to the word 'subsistence', and ensures that the vast majority of OAPs live in genuine poverty. The financial arrangements made for them by the State are predicated on the idea that, as you get older, your system slows down, so you don't need to eat.

Many impoverished OAPs have the decency to retreat to damp and gloomy basement flats where no one sees them (until a caring milkman, alerted by souring pints on the doorstep, pronounces them dead). Meanwhile, they can make endless cups of tea and huddle by paraffin fires, which is what old people enjoy. For an occasional treat, they open a tin of salmon or hobble down to the post-office. On a good day they catch a glimpse of that lovely Princess Diana on the telly. The sight of privileged young Royals spreading themselves around always bucks old people up.

I have not yet begun to fight . . .

AMERI-THINK: Death is optional. Or may be. At any rate, no point in lying down until you're dead. You owe it to yourself to maintain life at peak quality for as long as possible. If this means face-lifts or eyelid surgery or hair

transplants or 4 expensive weeks at the Pritikin Institute For Longevity ... go for it. If it means a new fur coat which simply makes you *feel* as if you'll live longer, then that's OK, too.

America's 'pensioners' are not automatically perceived as vulnerable and poor. The euphemistic phrase 'senior citizen' (Yanks won't tolerate anything less positive) calls to US minds a healthy older person in modest but comfortable circumstances. A lifetime of conscientious work has now made possible a Florida apartment, paid-up medical insurance, and regular long-distance 'phone calls to children and grandchildren in other cities. His/her reward in the skies (if not in heaven) is a special senior citizens' rate on cross-country air travel.

Ameri-pensioners in most social categories are obsessed by fitness and health. Naturally. It stands to reason that you have to take care of yourself if you're going to last. Observe on any Ameri-beach the jogging octogenarian, tanned to a deep shade of prune, and pausing only to pop a fistful of vitamin B-complex and yeast. He stopped smoking 20 years ago, and is now busy cutting all fats from his diet . . . 'keep the old arteries clean and you don't get senile'. He has cornered the world market in skimmed milk, virtually eliminated red meat, takes the skin off chicken and adds no butter to his steamed vegetables or morning wholemeal toast. He won't eat a pretzel without scraping the salt off first. His greatest fear in life is being caught somewhere where you can't get dental floss. He can reel off the name of virtually every carcinogen known to modern medicine, in between mouthfuls of bran. He sees life as a minefield of potential hazards for the elderly, which — with determination — he can sidestep. Avoid getting zapped, and the prize is — who knows — immortality! Sound crazy? Well, there are no guarantees in this life, and until someone comes up with a better theory, he's sticking to the one he's got.

17 A better class of foreigner

'Foreigner'

<u>**AMERI-THINK:**</u> Everybody in America is one, with the exception of half-a-dozen or so pure-blooded Sioux . . . which gets one problem out of the way. Having said that, there's no doubt that there are 'foreigners' and 'foreigners'. No matter how you slice it, a Brit is not as foreign as an Armenian, who is not as foreign as a Burmese, who is not as foreign as a Zulu.

In theory, America is the Great Melting Pot, where much is tolerated in terms of race, language, background, religion, and — goodness knows — cuisine. Only in America will any coffee shop sell you a kolbasi, an enchilada and a croissant to go.

But every culture has its sticking-points. Black people and Hispanics are still fighting for an even break, while people of Euro-extraction seem to have won one. 'Class A' orientals (the Japanese, and Hong Kong Chinese) are also doing well, with 'class B' orientals (Koreans, Filipinos, South-east Asians) moving up fast on the inside. Middle Europeans (Hungarians, Romanians, Czechs and Poles) fit in once they learn the lingo, and until then, play professional tennis. Yanks have no objection to Russian immigrants, who seem to do specially well in New York City, where they drive cabs and subvert only the traffic system. Israelis don't come to America, it's the other way around. Indians from India present a problem, because they are hard-working and desirable, but you don't want to open the floodgates; and Arabs are no problem because poor ones seldom come, and the rest head directly for the Mayo Clinic. Brits, Canadians, Aussies and people from Monte Carlo are classed as demi-foreigners.

While it is true that you must be born a US citizen if you wish to be President, non-native sons have been known to rise high. Ted Koppel (Born Brit) and Peter Jennings (Canadian) fill the small screen every night. Henry Kissinger — with traces of a German accent — was a power in the land, as was Zbigniew Brzezinski — though few could pronounce his name. To this day, no one knows if Lee Iacocca is American, Italian, or Japanese. One day, Rupert Murdoch will be President, even if he has to purchase the White House.

The foreign menace

BRIT-THINK: Brits are an insular people, who tend to stay put. They are physically and culturally homogeneous, and can spot outsiders miles off. Until relatively recently, Britain had no major influx of black or Asian immigrants, and therefore, no obvious target group to hate. Frustrated Yorkshiremen were forced to turn on Lancastrians as surrogate foreigners, and these local resentments have endured, even in the face of outside competition.

When non-whites appeared in significant numbers after the Second

---

British league-table of unreliable foreigners
(reading from *most* to *least* reliable)

Swiss
Have done very-nicely-thank-you by sitting on the fence. Are now running out of things to be neutral about. They lack humour, but are good at banks.

Americans
As Masters of the Planet, must be kept sweet. Would feel much better if we had 'dual key', and the guys in charge had grey matter.

Germans
If you forget the Second World War, and concentrate on up-market cars, electronics, fitted kitchens, and other things 'sprung technik'.

Swedes
Sexually deviant, drug-crazed, loony social ideas — but they do keep the place clean.

Japanese
Corporate zombies, not-like-us if you know what I mean, do anything for a yen but hard-working, and I love my Honda.

French/Italians/Spanish
Mad as hatters, utterly volatile and Catholic, which is the same thing. Swing right and left, change Governments like they change their socks. Only one stage removed from the real loonies ...

Libyans/Iranians/Irish/Palestinians
Proof, if any is needed, that whole nations can be clinically insane.

World War, Brits were faced with a problem: how to assimilate groups who had no obvious place in the class system? How to resist social fermentation, or — horror of horrors — *change*? So far, they have managed to keep chaos at bay. By some political slight-of-hand, immigrants have been consistently denied an effective power-base. Today, with non-whites forming a majority in many urban areas, Britain has no black or Asian MP (at the time of writing).

Brits repose no confidence in foreigners. Hyper-conscious of 'them' and 'us', they trust only 'us' . . . and 'us' is often limited to people they went to school with, or those born in the same street. Everyone else is unreliable. Non-Brits are *very* unreliable, and have no standards. Some Brits are more reliable than others, especially if they've been to good schools. People with manual jobs are sometimes reliable, but in their case, you call it 'honesty' or 'loyalty'.

In truth, Brits are mildly irritated by *all* foreigners . . . even white ones. They dislike the intrusion, the disruption to The System, and the tacit invitation to compare themselves with others — especially to their own detriment. As a rule, they do not feel inspired or motivated by unfamiliar ideas . . . they feel swamped and threatened.

So, they dislike Frenchmen ('Frogs'), Germans ('Krauts'), Yanks, Nips, and anyone else suspected of wanting to earn a living in the modern world. Xenophobia has reached record levels. This is why Brits are so keen on international football matches. They are perfect opportunities to beat up the other side's supporters for being foreign.

18 The Establishment

Whom, then, do Brits unreservedly love? They love entrenched members of THE ESTABLISHMENT. These are the people who have assured Brits for two generations that *Nothing Is Wrong* . . . despite all appearances to the contrary. They are, of course, society's winners; the 'I'm-Alright-Jack' set, with a stake in the status quo. They are fortunate in the character of the British proletariat, since average Brits are not inclined to follow malcontents with axes to grind — even when provoked, frustrated or impoverished. They're content to allow 'top people' to run the show, as long as wage-packets keep rough pace with inflation, and the Clapham Omnibus runs on time.

If the Establishment's track record is less than dazzling, it is nevertheless unchallenged. Brit-prol is not by nature revolutionary — (or even *evolutionary*) — and generally takes the view that 'better the devil you know'. There's a world-weary acceptance of Empires lost, opportunities unfulfilled. Would-be political agitators have ever found that Brits are civilized pessimists, given to constant recrimination — but no action. Top People are utterly safe, and can rest easy . . . if they can stand the carping.

Yanks — who lack Brit-radar — may be hard-pressed to identify members of said Establishment. By definition, these are the Chosen People at the apex of the class system. Appearances can deceive, since they may have money or may not; but what they all share is *influence*. Many were born great, some had greatness thrust upon them, and a very few achieved greatness.

Indeed, the definition is fairly vague in Brit-minds. Some refer to 'the Establishment', and mean anyone who votes Tory and earns more than £20,000 a year. Some narrow it down to power-brokers — people with real political clout, like captains of industry, Fleet Street proprietors, and cousins to the Queen. There are, of course, worrying grey areas. Is Bob Geldof a member of the Establishment, or not? If in doubt, try this simple litmus test:

In a Brit-society so cruelly divided into 'winners' and 'losers', they do not have a genuine stake in the 'winners' side.

Clive is never very busy these days. Fortunately his money is.

AMERI-THINK: In one sense, virtually *everyone* in America is THE ESTABLISHMENT, with the possible exception of migrant workers and people on welfare. The Consensus Society is full of people with a personal stake in the system; committed to making it bigger and better, then taking a hefty cut. If you want to increase your equity (and average Yanks do), increase the market.

To this extent, trade unionists are the Establishment. Farmers and stockbrokers, artists and writers are the Establishment. In the Ramboized Eighties, students are *certainly* the Establishment.

With political dissent virtually absent, all participants expect a piece of the action. Of course, Yanks will admit that some get a bigger piece than others . . . and, though billed as 'the classless society', America has a large — and growing — Super Establishment. This is the Power Elite — the people who call the shots; who have the money and influence to make elected leaders responsive to their needs. In short, they're the ones who Have It All. Here's how to recognize them:

America's Haute-Establishment — Anyone who:

1 is unduly pre-occupied with the latest rulings on tax-shelters
2 has stopped *buying* 'how to' books, and started *writing* them
3 has ever played golf in the Bob Hope Classic
4 buys drug items at regular price
5 toys with the food at yet another $1,000-a-plate fundraising dinner, then eats an omelette at home
6 has homes and cars on both coasts
7 is racking up 'frequent travellers' miles' with three separate airlines
8 has a nutritionist, a broker, an accountant, a lawyer, a shrink, a housekeeper and a personal 'trainer', and is considering a press agent
9 owns several furs, but spends half the year in hot climates
10 operates a McDonald's franchise
11 has personal and corporate AMEX platinum cards, and gets letters of congratulations for frequent use
12 lost money with John DeLorean.

19 Goods and services

Consumer durables and vice versa

BRIT-THINK: Because the British feel guilty when life is too easy, Brit-consumers like — and buy — things which present a challenge. Manufacturers cater for this quirk in the national character by producing a range of products which don't entirely work. Or, sort of work. Sometimes.

Specially popular are expensive, domestically-made toasters which miraculously burn bread on one side, while leaving the other side raw. This is a master-stroke of mechanical and marketing genius. Brits, it seems, do not like automatic and uniformly good results. They hate being outclassed by machines, preferring to feel involved, and *necessary*. Technical perfection worries them. Given the chance, they purchase 'friendly' items, which have shortcomings, and need human intervention: frying-pans with hard-to-reach corners which trap food; twin-tub washing machines, which require users to do half the work by hand. These give consumers a sense of purpose.

Many Brits are not at one with science. They are skeptical about modern technology, and feel gratified when doubts are confirmed by experience. Mechanical fallibility restores their faith in human beings, their love for nature, and gives them a chance to laugh at those who over-reach themselves by inventing smart gadgets. Brits are so relieved and have such a chuckle when things go wrong.

Ad agencies take careful note of such reactions, and time after time produce brilliant campaigns, admirably tailored to Brit-psyches. In brief, it's the classic British under-sell; and products must be portrayed as short on technology, long on natural goodness (and/or connection with the countryside). Ads for a new cake-mix never claim 'perfect results every time!' This rules out the possibility of failure, and does not underscore the importance of the human contribution or the 'naturalness' of the product. Far better, 'perfect country cakes, 9 times out of 10!' Know thy customer. It'll sell and sell.

In any case, Brits are perverse enough to shun goods which are the subject of extravagant claims. They pride themselves on being too smart to fall for hype. They do not rush — as Yanks do — to buy 'the best/the brightest/the softest' item on the market, preferring a low-key approach. 'Dazzle — not bad for a fabric whitener' makes them love the product. It has so little to live up to. And consumer criticism is utterly defused by the clever 'British Rail ... We're Getting There'.

Conspicuous Ameri-consumption:

Americans are quite simply the best consumers in the world ... the most enthusiastic and experienced. They'll consume carefully or conspicuously, but consume they must — and on a regular basis. No wonder a famous American T-shirt reads, 'Whoever Has The Most Things When He Dies Wins.' Yanks — indisputably the best-equipped people in the world — hedge constantly against the possibility of shortage. They seem to need a lot of stuff. That's why, when they find something they like, they buy 'in multiples' — i.e., several of the same thing in different colours. They do this with La Coste sports shirts featuring alligators on the pockets. They do it with cashmere sweaters and leather loafers. When in doubt, Yanks will always purchase, on the grounds that it never hurts to have another one of anything, but you may be sorry *not* to. They are the only people in the world overheard re-assuring each other in department stores, 'Buy, buy. So you'll *have* an extra raincoat.'

Yanks are also the most *receptive* consumers on earth. Brits may think

123

them credulous and gullible, but the truth is that they *believe* in products. First of all, they are culturally pre-disposed to think that 'new is good', and 'newer is better'. Hooked on the idea of progress and growth, they're convinced that the quality of life is susceptible to all kinds of improvement. Hence, they embrace technological (if not political) change. There's an underlying assumption that research solves problems . . . and you, too, can benefit from the latest developments.

It follows that Yanks love the word 'now'. 'Crunchie's Cornflakes — *now* fortified with iron'; 'aspirin . . . *now* coated for stomach protection'; 'diet cola — *now* 97% caffeine-free'. Copywriters know that the word can boost sales by up to 25%. There's public confidence that, if someone bothered to change it, they must've made it better.

Society, Americans believe, is only as good as the technology — and the solutions — it produces. Very often, they're one and the same thing. Look at the Salk vaccine. Look at the silicon chip, or Star Wars. Furthermore (and this precept is fundamental to Ameri-think) ALL PROBLEMS CAN BE SOLVED. That's why they do it at the end of each episode of *The A-Team*, or *Cagney and Lacey* or *Hotel*. They're just as

optimistic about the energy crisis, a cure for heart-disease, and the Irish problem. All it takes, they're convinced, is determination ... and, if one method fails, a new approach. People who resist change are perceived as lazy, rigid, or — even worse — elderly. This is the country of 'can do', and Yanks are self-congratulatory about their attitude. They like to begin sentences with the catch-phrase, 'only in America'. 'Only in America would scientists spend $14 million developing a special aerosol container, so astronauts can swig Pepsi in outer space.'

Attacking the problem

Brit-tendency is to beaver away at the periphery of a problem, hoping some day to arrive at the centre. Americans prefer to identify the heart and aim first at that, leaving side-issues to resolve themselves. But, something in the British character and nature feels happiest with an oblique approach. It's not that Brits don't understand what needs to be done. It's not that they can't identify priorities. They can — but something gets in the way ... a built-in resistance to direct action, and radical solutions. Some say that they lack a 'killer' instinct. This may be because *solving* a problem inevitably means change; tampering with the trend of events, and cutting up rough. Often, Brits opt instead for a cosmetic operation. For example: if the problem is massive and widespread youth unemployment, Brits will fund a camping and adventure scheme for inner-city kids. If major city hospitals are overcrowded and under-resourced, stop-gap measures will encourage pregnant women to give birth at home. Brits perpetually rush to plug dikes and contain disasters, without confronting causes.

This is partly, of course, a question of economics ... but not entirely. The Brit-approach is never revolutionary — and they are flummoxed when required to wipe the slate clean, and start again, much prefering to 'hang in there, and make the best of a bad job'.

Example:

A huge urban housing-project takes many years to build. As the first stage is completed, certain problems become apparent: i.e., heating isn't powerful enough, water-pressure's too low, insufficient laundry facilities for residents.

Yanks will:

1   attempt to rectify problems in Stage Two
2   go back and improve Stage One as time and money permits.

Brits will:

1   complete the entire project as planned
2   then go back and correct all the mistakes: 'it's fairer to everyone'.

In classic, fundamental Brit-think, when something begins to go wrong, you *keep doing it*. This is called 'perpetuation of mistakes'. To change mid-way is irresponsible, 'un-British'. One must see things through. It's a sort of technological charge of the Light Brigade. It also accounts for:

1   the development of a national telephone system which wholly failed to standardize area-codes. Users dial different (and unpredictable) numbers of digits for every area in the country
2   an electrical system which makes impossible the sale of goods complete with standardized plugs for standardized outlets
3   milk delivered to families only in space-wasting pints, and never in quart containers
4   heavy coin currency in small denominations (2p, 10p) which wears out pockets and weighs down handbags. Then, the introduction of unconvincing pound coins which quickly get lost.

BRIT-SELL:
AMERI-SELL:

British and American sales personnel are present in stores for entirely different reasons. Yanks are there to increase their take-home pay by making commission on sales. In this, they are helped by their store's inventory policy. Let's take women's fashions. If a customer sees something she likes, chances are that it can be found in stock in her size, her colour. *If not*, it can be located at a nearby branch, and sent to her branch free of charge. *If not*, her branch will 'special order' her choice direct from the manufacturer. One way or another, the sales person will get the item and make the sale, even if she has to walk to the warehouse. After all — she has 3% riding on it.

British salespeople are very attached to merchandise, and try hard to keep it in the store. They will not part with goods unless forced. For example, if you ask for a particular size, they will:

1   ignore you
2   point in the direction of a rack across the floor, without breaking off their conversation long enough to acknowledge you
3   snap, 'if it's not out, we haven't got it'.

If you positively *insist* on buying something, the in-store system will force you to queue for ages at a crowded till in order to pay for it. They'll take even longer to OK the purchase on your credit card, so as to discourage you for next time. And they will never, *ever* agree to refund or credit anything, unless threatened with the full weight of the law. Brit salespeople believe in strong deterrents for recidivist shoppers . . . and they make sure that the punishment fits the purchase. They are visibly relieved if you just go away. They're not, after all, there to sell. They are there to talk with colleagues about last night's date, and you are bothering them.

BRIT-SHOP:
AMERI-SHOP:

Brits are somewhat oppressed — even intimidated — by salespeople, and tend to shop apologetically. They don't like to be trouble to anyone: 'Awfully sorry to bother you . . . do you have this in a size 8?' Men suffer particularly from shopo-phobia, and will do anything to avoid contact — never mind confrontation. They are obedient and inhibited customers. In shops, they rush to purchase the first garment or pair of shoes produced, and hate asking to try other sizes or styles. They shop only when forced by circumstances, and never for pleasure. They are push-overs as consumers, since they will buy *anything* — literally — just to get out of the shop.

Brits are mortally embarrassed by salespeople. This is because, being polite people, they have never learned how to say 'no' to them. They buy things they don't want because they lack the finesse required to extricate themselves from situations. And, since they *know* they'll be trapped, they avoid entering shops altogether. Even normally dynamic Brits are utterly compliant customers . . . putty in the hands of M&S's most junior assistant. Their mouths cannot form the crucial series of one-syllable words, 'no-thanks-I-don't-like-it'. Salespeople know this, and exploit the advantage . . . taking Brit-consumer's money, secure in the knowledge that they'll never, ever be asked to give it back.

Yanks, as the world's most dedicated consumers, sport a series of

127

shopping-related badges and bumper-stickers which read:

1 WHEN THE GOING GETS TOUGH, THE TOUGH GO SHOPPING
2 WHO SHOPS WINS
3 IF YOU THINK MONEY CAN'T BUY HAPPINESS, YOU'VE BEEN SHOPPING IN THE WRONG PLACES
4 SHOPPING IS MY EVEREST
5 MORE IS MORE

There is nothing more satisfying to them than the sense of achievement and *control* that comes with Purchase Power. There is nothing so gratifying as a good fight in a store — which they inevitably win, since America's customer is always right. American women fight for recreation in Saks much as they play tennis or visit museums.

They have no psychological problem with salespeople, who are there to serve. They address them without embarrassment, since, in America, everyone's selling something anyway. Yes, everyone shops, and shopping is the Great Equalizer. It's the Consensus Society extended to the Consumer Society.

For Yanks, shopping also has a healing and therapeutic effect. Shops are where you fantasize about the future, and try it on for size. They're where you put the present together, a piece at a time. If life is about Having It All, shops are where you get It. But, most important of all, shopping is about *control* . . . i.e., if it's my money, I get to get what I want. Including the treatment I think I deserve. Stores are places where money puts *you* in charge, and you can make sure you get what's coming to you. When you shop, you should ideally purchase victory. It's good for the soul.

20 Doctor Doctor

Medicine

American medical care is absurdly expensive, and unavailable to the poor ... but works.

The British National Health Service is moderately priced, and available to everyone ... but doesn't.

Nowhere is the gulf between Brit and Ameri-think more pronounced than in the area of medicine. Attitudes to health and doctors say much about perceptions of self — and the individual's place in the scheme of things. When it comes to expectation of care, priorities and results — in fact, when it comes to matters of life and death — Brits and Yanks are poles apart.

Britain's National Health Service is predicated on the idea that medical resources are strictly limited. In the name of fairness, they must be allocated — and priorities determined — by the State. To each according to his need, and so on. Brits believe that first-class public health-care is the foundation of a civilized society ... but the 'first class' bit presents problems. Quality costs money, and too often already limited supply is forced to meet growing demand ... with the result that patients virtually draw straws for time on kidney machines.

Hence, the NHS has come to co-exist in parallel with a private health service, based in London's Harley Street. Here, senior consultants called 'Mr' instead of 'Dr' vie with each other to see who can combine the dingiest waiting-room with the steepest prices. This is where the well-heeled come to enjoy the comforts of second-hand furniture and circumvent a hopelessly clogged public system.

Brits are tormented by the very existence of this private sector, fearing that a 'two-tier' system creates double standards, in which the poor are bound to lose out. Thus, there is constant pressure for the abolition of said private sector, and the creation of a single tier, in which everyone loses out.

Policy within the overstretched NHS itself is, of necessity, to put the 'needs of the community' first ('we-think'), and individual requirements second. Emergencies are treated as such, but it's up to doctors — never patients — to decide what's an emergency and what isn't. There's no appeal, unless you wish to change doctors. In any case, Brit consumers of public health-care feel honour-bound to wait their turn. Thousands of thirsty elephants move to the rear, while those in greatest need take a turn at the water-hole first. Hard to say, in the end, who needs a drink most. Thus it occasionally happens that the NHS kills off individuals while raising overall public health standards.

In both sectors Brits have strange notions of the professional relationship between doctor and patient. It can be most nearly described as . . . hero-worship. Doc is doing The Great I Am. It's Great Healer vs. Unquestioning Recipient. There's a view amongst doctors — and subscribed to by patients — that a body is not for the lay person. Your own is none of your business, and should be dealt with only by outside professionals.

If you've a pain (and no doubt you'll be *hopeless* at explaining it properly) The Doctor will tell you what it is. (He'll use the patronizing pseudo prol-talk they taught him at medical school . . . i.e., 'you've got gastro-enteritis. That's basically a pain in the gut.') Then he'll prescribe something for it, the contents of which should not concern you. Don't

ask. He takes the view that a little bit of knowledge is a dangerous thing. Brit-patient is meant to be just that.

It must be said, however, that to some extent, Brit-consumers of medical care get what they deserve. Many apparently well-educated people are clueless about physiology. They've acquired no understanding of the body, or how it works. They don't know a gall bladder from an epiglottis, and really do believe that the head-bone's connected to the stomach-bone: 'I've got a vaginal discharge, doctor. Do you think it's my sinuses?'

Moi first, doc

Yanks belong to the 'me, first' school of medicine. They have few ethical and moral dilemmas about:

1 who should pay
2 priorities, and
3 limited resources.

They know the answer to (1), which more or less obviates (2) and (3).

When it comes to medicine, Yank-think is crystal-clear. *You* are your own best friend and first priority. Otherwise, all bets are off, and all considerations meaningless — because you're dead. Even if your problem is an ingrown hangnail, we're talking quality-of-life here, and your need is as great as the next guy's. After all, if *you* don't look after Number One and all the little Number One-ettes, who will? And if you're selfless enough to take a back-seat, where's your reward? In heaven? Nuts.

Furthermore — demand high standards. The threat of a malpractice suit provides leverage, and keeps doc on his toes. In the Yank medical canon, there's no such thing as 'no fault' — or, as Brits put it — 'verdict: misadventure'. Americans do not *believe* in accident. There may, perhaps, be absence of malice ... but, basically, if somebody goofed, then somebody's gonna pay.

All Yanks are back-seat doctors ... informed and demanding. They feel entitled to a second guess, and a third opinion. If Doc wants his fee, he'll endure the third degree from patients who've read dozens of Sunday Magazine articles on hardening of the arteries, or the long-term effects of Cortisone. He expects to explain *why* he's prescribing a broad-spectrum anti-biotic, or *why* cystitis is not indicated. Then Yank-patient looks it all up in the comprehensive AMA-endorsed medical dictionary he keeps

Well Irving, your Xray looks okay to me – what do you think?

at home (on the bedside table), and calls back if he wishes to question the diagnosis, or review his symptoms.

Doctors

AMERI-THINK: A doctor is a necessary evil . . . a man in a white coat who gets you when you're down, over-medicates, operates at the drop of a chin-line and uses your misfortunes to pad his annual income. Watch him like a hawk. Ask plenty of questions, and don't let him near you with a wet cotton-swab unless:

    1   it's a matter of life-and-death
    2   you've had a second opinion
    3   you've negotiated his fee.

Remember that you can never win in any encounter with the medical profession. The rule is simple, and the odds are on their side. They get the money, but the results are never guaranteed.

BRIT-THINK: Respect all medical men and women, dedicated servants of the community. Overworked healers with a sense of vocation, bleary-eyed with sleepless hours of service to mankind. Do *not* ask too many questions. Your case is paltry, and your life one tiny speck of light in the doctor's vast fermament. Anyway — being challenged or called to account or asked what's in a prescription seems to annoy him.

Perfect Brit patients

British patients are *all* perfect — and very well-behaved. This is because they are terrified of British doctors. Model patients who wish to further improve performance will be careful:

1 never to get sick at weekends, or after office-hours. Not only is the doctor annoyed, but your neighborhood chemist has shut in sympathy.
2 not to live alone. When you're ill, there'll be no one to take you to the doctor's. He hates making house-calls, and reasons that if you're *really* sick, you'll make an effort to come to him. If confined to bed, you'll need a friend to collect prescriptions from the chemist, who will not deliver.
3 to ask no questions. About anything. Display no familiarity with medical terms or generic drugs. Do not inquire about side-effects (in the case of medications) or risks (in the case of surgery) . . . much less the percentage chances of success.
4 never to need something *major*, like a heart-transplant. His heart isn't in it. This counts as 'crisis' medicine, and many Brit-docs consider that scarce NHS resources can be better deployed in improving general standards of care than in keeping just one person (you) alive. It will be hard for you to share this view.
5 never to bother the hospital nurses, or ring the bedside bell. It may distract them from something really urgent, like a NUPE/COSHE meeting.
6 if having a baby, never to praise midwives to doctors, or vice versa. They loathe each other, and have long-standing rivalries about who should do episiotomies, and who gets to suture. Just keep your head down, and make sure the new-born does likewise.
7 not to look closely at hospital decor (which causes clinical depression). Try not to think about Legionnaires' Disease.
8 to ignore the tatty squalor of your GP's office. Cast from your mind rules of basic hygiene. Try not to shiver in the draughts. On no account think about AIDS, and pretend not to notice that he used the same thermometer on the last patient, and you didn't see him clean it.

9 *never* to ask for a check-up. Preventative medicine is an 'American' idea (Brit-docs are Yanko-phobes) and is associated in his mind with hypochondria. He much prefers to see you when it's far too late. At least that way, he knows it's *real*.

10 not to mention American medicine at all, unless you wish to trigger a violent episode. Brit-doc cannot decide which to disparage first:

(a) the huge incomes of his Ameri-colleagues, or

(b) the huge malpractice suits awarded against them.

His professional nightmare is that one day, model Brit-patients will turn nasty, and wake up to the possibilities of (b) when he hasn't enough of (a) to support it.

The perfect Ameri-patient

... NEED DO ONLY ONE IMPORTANT THING: stay conscious long enough to sign the medical insurance forms. Ameri-doctor seems to work with greater skill and sense of Hypocratic vocation when he knows you carry Blue Cross, Blue Shield and Major Medical.

21 Laws of the lands

Britain and America use roughly the same judicial system to dispense roughly the same rough justice. There are, however, certain practical and philosophical differences. Brits have a 'split profession' — solicitors and barristers — which has the effect of giving consumers one lawyer for the price of two.

> SCENARIO:
> Brit-client takes his problem to a solicitor, who doesn't know the answer. He, in turn, 'takes advice from counsel' — i.e., consults a specialist barrister — who doesn't know the answer, but looks it up in a big book, then tells it to the solicitor, who tells it to the client. Then they both charge the client.

Yank lawyers do not operate in the same way, and hate the idea of dividing the spoils. They contrive to keep most specialist work within the firm ... whether clients want a simple divorce, or plan to sue NASA for third stage burn-out pollution over Missouri.

The most significant thing to know about top-earning American lawyers, is that they do not want to practise. What they want is to jockey for position and end up on the inside track in some great business deal which will make them a quick million. Law school is simply a means to this end. Socially conscious grads bury themselves in civil rights work, or a D.A.'s office. Other high-flyers soon find everyday bread-and-butter work dull and tedious (few thrills in corporate tax law) and secretly wish that they worked in television. They alleviate the boredom by:

1 skipping the small stuff. Delegating nearly everything (your case) to overworked juniors, keeping themselves fresh and alert in case a lucrative 'class action' comes along. This is known as striking the mother-lode. Nouveau avocat can smell a class action miles away (i.e., third stage burn-out pollution over Missouri).

2 charging ridiculously inflated fees for services. Jaded Yank-lawyer can artificially arouse his own interest only if his fee runs to six figures. This is a form of professional masturbation.
3 attending frequent American Bar Association conventions, which offer a chance to thrash out with colleagues such ethical and moral dilemmas as which is the best restaurant/shirt-maker in London.

Criminal cases in particular are treated differently on opposite sides of the water. This is because of separate understandings of the vexed question of guilt and innocence. In both countries, the defendant is technically innocent until proven guilty; but there the similarities cease. If Brit-client (about to be tried for a crime) confides to his lawyer that he *did* it (i.e., 'I shot Fred') then counsel is duty-bound to advise him to plead guilty — albeit with mitigating circumstances ... (i.e., 'I fired in self-defence'). The consideration of guilt or innocence is *settled*, and purely objective: if the defendant did it, regardless of circumstances, then he/she is technically guilty. (The question of intent may come later.)

Yanks don't buy that. As far as they're concerned, guilt is a subjective thing ... as is criminal intent. If there are doubts, or extenuating circumstances, then you're technically innocent — which is how you should plead. Even if you fired the gun. If you're guilty, let the Prosecution prove it. That's what he's paid for.

In civil matters, it is well-known that Americans love to go to court. They will happily litigate at the drop of a contract-clause. Suing is a national sport, second only to baseball ... and everyone can play, including incarcerated criminals (who have been known to sue their lawyers, the State, and even their *victims* from the confines of prison). When Yanks run out of reasons to go to court, they invent new ones — like palimony suits.

This is of course costly, but — because of the high level of Ameri-damages — can also be extremely profitable. Just ask the TV producer who collected $300,000 because his name was accidentally dropped from the list of credits at the end of a programme. Compensation in America is exactly that. It makes up for everything.

Not so in Britain, where the most frightful mishaps can be put down to 'misadventure' — i.e., accident, where no fault or negligence attaches, and no compensation applies. Even successful suits attract small levels of damages (Brits don't like to 'encourager les autres'). Courts will award around £34,000 top whack for an unmitigated disaster with malice aforethought.

This means that there's not much incentive to sue, grabbit and run, either for Brit-clients or lawyers. No one can afford to take chances. Professional codes of conduct prohibit lawyers from accepting cases on a contingency basis; it is felt that, to do so smacks of 'profiteering'. This places civil proceedings off-limits for average Brits, and means that, in order to bring an action in a UK court, the client must be:

1   very rich (he can afford to pay up, whatever the outcome)
2   very poor (he'll get legal aid)
3   a lawyer himself.

In fact, Britain's Law Society resists every attempt by the profession to drag itself into the twentieth century. Not only do governing legal eagles instinctively *detest* change, but they are much too clever to endanger a cosy cartel in the name of a fairer deal for consumers. For instance, they would rather hang up their silks than allow commercial advertising — with the risk of competitive pricing of services which is implied. If a Brit-lawyer wishes to covertly advertise for custom, he is hardly flamboyant. He places a 'change of address' notice in a suitable trade publication.

Needless to say, Yank lawyers have few restrictions and fewer inhibitions along these lines. They shamelessly chase every opportunity.

137

'Find an ambulance,' the saying goes, 'and the lawyer will be close behind.' This is called creative suing. And every night, American TV viewers are bombarded with ads for legal services:

> Hello! Have you suffered an industrial accident? ... Are you *sure*? ... Do you know anyone *else* who's been injured ... Would you *like* to be injured?
> Then how about a divorce?

Anyone who rises to the bait can shop around for the lowest prices — then charge it all on MasterCard.

22 Pets

Anglo-Ameri-pets

Household pets have long been popular in both Britain and America . . . playthings for affluent societies. Non-working animals which have to be fed remain luxuries for the relatively rich (not many poodles in Ethiopia) and whole menageries are for the relatively richer. Private zoos and safari parks exist all over Britain, and in some parts of Hollywood (where there are lots of animals).

For Anglo-American animal lovers, pets are diversions and objects of affection. They are also fashion accessories which say as much about an owner's style and aspirations as the clothes he/she wears, the books read, the music listened to. Speak, Rover.

That is why, without question, *dogs* are man's best friend. It's said that elderly ladies prefer cats, that rock-stars take iguanas for walks on leashes and sailors talk most openly to parrots. But dogs most nearly reflect and then *project* their owners' personalities. Both Brit and Yank owners know precisely how to 'say it with Rover'.

AMERI-POOCH: . . . is the best friend of a conspicuous consumer. Time was ('round about the Fifties) when Yanks in the fast lane just *had* to have poodles. Budding starlets walked them on Hollywood Boulevard, where it was chic'er still to dye them pink. The colour matched your outfit, your bedroom or your eyes, and demonstrated to the world that you were successful enough to afford the grooming charges.

Today, virtually any pooch can complete your image, or tell your story. You're free to walk a Schnauzer or a Great Dane or a Chitzu with a bow in its hair. Even a friendly mutt with one white eye and a floppy ear says much about your casual, blue-denim style.

Just as telling are the *names* Americans give their pets. 'Ralph' to suggest the unpretentious mongrel found in an alleyway; 'Spago' for

Beverly Hills pup, named after the town's grooviest restaurant; 'Bismark' for a Dachshund with an educated owner.

Yanks who want to 'Have It All' do not cut corners when it comes to Rover. They'll splash out on poodle parlours with pet saunas and herbal baths, or top vets with high-tech surgeries ... offering laser treatment, vitamins, plastic surgery (ears pinned back for a self-conscious Cocker) and doggie TV featuring remote-control channel-changer ('he just loves *Dynasty*, and we never watch it').

... And, yes, doggie psychiatry. Barry Manilow really did have his beagle, Bagel, analysed.

Ameri-pet may even carry the burden of his owner's fantasies. Some Yanks enjoy casting their pets as heroes; sort of furry 4-legged Clint Eastwoods or Charles Bronsons (who is pretty furry already). Hence the popularity of Lassie, Rin Tin Tin and Wonder Dog. It's not enough for Ameri-dog merely to lick his owner, and chew on an old slipper. He's also got to save the world.

BRIT-DOG: ... has one major aspirational function. This is to help his owner to live out the 'Country Life' fantasy, which suggests sprawling estates with people in tweeds and plenty of animals. Brit-pooch is the 'plenty of animals'. (This is no mean achievement when you live in a basement flat in Putney.) Nothing daunted, Brit-owner will don woollens and wellies for a walk with Fido across open heath (or failing that, a grass verge will do) emerging at the corner Indian grocery for a pint of milk. Fido does his bit by barking away, pretending to be a brace of dogs on a double lead, hot on the scent of something countrified ... but spoils the illusion by sniffing at every Mars Bar wrapper on the pavement.

Brit-dog has few luxuries in this life, like grooming parlours and gourmet dinners. No one follows him around with a gold-plated pooper-scooper; he's lucky if he's had his injections, and been de-wormed. He certainly doesn't boast a poncey name, and is likely to answer to 'Blackie' or 'Spot' or 'Tim'. But his owner loves him (often better than people), and lets him chew on scraps of fresh rabbit, and likes it best when he shakes them all over the quarry-tiled floor of the kitchen, because it conjures up visions of great liver-coloured dogs in great stone-floored halls near great hearths on great country estates far, far from Balham.

Brit-dog is not hero; he is _hunter_. His owner likes to dream of him following a carefully-laid aniseed trail, or savaging a fox. (In fact, he is more likely to savage a soft ginger-biscuit, or the family cat.) Brits also adore sheep-dogs. Britain is probably the only country on earth which could run TV sheep-dog trials in prime time, and get soap-sized ratings. What Joan Collins is to Yanks' fantasies, sheep-dogs are to Brits'.

141

23 Judging a nation by its television

Meet the Press:
The media we deserve

It's always dangerous to make snap-judgements about someone else's television. Brits criticize the American product for being intellectually negligible and crass; Yanks regard much UK output as slow, worthy and turgid. But prolonged TV viewing is a wonderful key to national attitudes.

It should be said that — although we feel we are well-acquainted with each other's TV — we are not. Most Brits base their opinions of America's vast news and entertainment service on:

1 buy-ins screened in the UK
2 a few hours' sporadic viewing at a motel near LA airport.

Similarly, Yanks form impressions of Brit-progs by dipping in and out of the (intellectually rarified) PBS network. When in London, they may catch a special on *Birds of Britain*, or *One Man And His Dog* in prime time. These are not regarded as compulsive viewing. Then, after 1.30 a.m., all is darkness.

AMERI-TV: First, there's lots of it. Americans believe in super-abundant choice, and see no reason why TV should be an exception to the rule. Second (and as a result), it is competitive ... with dozens of channels chasing a limited — if large — number of viewers. Success depends on attracting attention. Programmes need to make a splash; ditto personalities. (In a country with 230 million people, you can't be quiet and expect the culture to recognize you.)

So: the first 90 seconds of your station's new sit-com must be the freshest, the funniest, the sexiest. A cops 'n robbers series better be the most thrilling and dangerous, with nary a wasted frame. Girls must be pretty. Men must be handsome. Ameri-audiences have learned to expect instant gratification, and there are no second chances. Even producers of high-quality current affairs are at pains to satisfy popular tastes. Disappoint the viewer, and other worlds are his at the touch of a remote-control button: from feature films on cable, to MTV, to rolling news, soft porn or repeats of *Mork and Mindy*. This is the video equivalent of 'Having It All'. The result is that makers of American television have created rods for their own backs by creating Ameri-viewer. Over-stimulated, restless and skittish, he typically has the attention-span of an ant (research shows maximum 3 mins). His ability to concentrate is shot.

Zap, Zap, Zap! To say you had the attention span of an ant would be insulting to ants.

BRIT-TELLY: Brits confuse TV in general (and the BBC in particular) with morality in general and goodness in particular. They are never sure where entertainment fits in, let alone commerce . . . and grapple hopelessly with these issues every time the licence-fee comes up for renewal.

To resolve the confusion, they have set up 'watchdog' bodies (rough equivalents to America's FCC) to monitor broadcasting, and make sure that no one enjoys it too much. Part of their job is to limit competition (i.e., the number of stations on the air) and to interfere as much as possible with the ones they've got. As a result, no one knows whether British TV is:

1　a branch of Government and/or the Home Office
2　electronic Moral Example (a branch of the Church of England)
3　just another means of selling toothpaste
4　an adventure playground for 'creative' adults (e.g., journalists and producers) who would be a nuisance and virtually unemployable elsewhere.

Brit TV executives pride themselves on intellectual and creative integrity. They are, they claim, above the ignoble American scramble for ratings. They do not pander to viewers accustomed to 'instant nirvana', and are fully prepared to give new programmes a chance to 'run in'. Nor are they slaves to the sudden-death ratings-system known as 'overnights'. (They can't *afford* overnights.) Success, they claim, is not about 'popularity'. In truth, they see programme content as some reflection of the quality of their own minds, and do not wish to be judged harshly. This presents problems when considering *Game For A Laugh*.

But what really annoys Brit TV moguls is the thought that 'formula' American programmes — often high on lip-gloss and low on IQ — have consistently swept the boards in Britain. Brit-viewer (accustomed as he is to Finer Things) has not proved immune to the charm of *Charlie's Angels*. This seems like a betrayal, but does nothing to *change* (there's that word again) programming policy. It merely proves that viewer flesh is contemptibly weak. Also, that Yanks have mastered the trick of producing images and stories deeply satisfying to a broad public (no mean achievement). Brit-moguls could, of course, refuse to *buy* them; but that would be commercial suicide. Instead, they compromise by showing them and being snooty about them at the same time. Brit-viewers, for their part, have rapidly acquired more video cassette recorders per capita than any other country in the world except Japan, and use them to watch American films.

Ameri-vision:
You are what you watch

Yanks have few philosophical problems with television. They have more or less resolved the conundrum about combining hard news investigation with ads for Toyotas. At bottom, they're confident that programme *quantity* finally ensures fairness and quality ... and this is a safety-net. If the 'ignoble scramble for ratings' produces some naff daytime soaps and pretty thin sit-coms, it's also brought us *M.A.S.H.* and *Bilko*, and Ted Koppel and Edward R. Murrow. Most important, Yanks see television as a business first of all, and a public utility second. No network presumes to appoint itself guardian of public morals, and arbiter of taste. That's *your* job.

Brit-TV:
They're watching me

Brit programme-makers are often hampered in their jobs by the Brit Establishment's (see Chapter 18) photo-phobia. Power-brokers (politicians apart) often regard the camera as enemy, and do not like being watched. The impact of pictures transmitted direct to the public is random, dangerous ... impossible to judge. Where possible, Great British Public is prohibited from receiving its information 'neat'. So, cameras are excluded from:

1 courts of law. (reporters are compelled to *sketch* pictures of the proceedings instead)
2 the House of Commons. (where necessary, the nightly news shows slides of MPs — or the debating chamber — combined with audio recordings)
3 wars. (when Brit-troops engaged the Argies in the Falklands, reporters were asked to leave their cameras in Shepherd's Bush)

Yanks love cameras, and basically feel that *nothing is real* unless it exists on video. I Vide(o), Therefore I Am. Andy Warhol struck an all-American chord when he said that everyone should be famous for 15 minutes. The Press has instant access to events and people, with only the inner recesses of the Pentagon and the CIA generally off-limits. This can lead to press scrums, and the abandonment of all acceptable standards of behaviour when the heat is on (witness TWA Beirut hostage crisis). On the 'plus' side, it has also led to Watergate, and to demands for the present Freedom of Information laws, which increase the Government's accountability to Ameri-public. TV transforms reality.

You are what you read

... And Brits read lots. Many leaf through 7 or 8 national 'dailies' every morning, then a collection of weeklies, trade-mags and evening papers later on. Not to mention the give-aways. Brits are voracious consumers of printed matter ... and fast readers.

Newspapers have long thrived in the UK; first, because Brits are literate people, and second, because geography is on Fleet Street's side. For the past 100 years, this relatively small country has been served by a sophisticated rail network. Papers printed in London can be distributed to the far corners of the realm on the same day. And in recent decades, Britain's well-developed popular press has used this natural advantage to disseminate stories of national importance, such as:

1 'Registered Nurse Turns Vice Girl'
2 'When Hell Broke Out At Church Bash'
3 'Pop Star's Secret Wedding Confession To His Bride'
4 'Girl's Sex-Slave Nightmare With Killer Optician'

Britain's national papers are, of course, divided into two categories:

The quality press, or 'posh' papers
(you know it's 'posh' if you can't turn its pages in a crowded commuter train without assaulting the passenger next to you).

The 'popular press', or tabloids
(anything of more manageable size, with a nude on page 3, and £1 million Bingo Jackpots everywhere else).

America has quality papers and rags, too ... but there are subtle differences in style.

1 **Brit tabloids are more explicit.**

Yanks read their own hugely popular *National Enquirer* because — as the ad says — they 'want to know'. But they don't find out. At least, not *everything*. When visiting the UK, even hardened *Enquirer* readers blush at the intimate detail in the popular press. Reports of a rape case will leave nothing to the imagination. Readers will *know* how many times he had entry.

2   *Brit papers declare political affiliations.*

US papers merely hint at these, maintaining the appearance of objectivity (though regular readers know precisely where they stand). Brit-papers abandon pretence, and nail political colours firmly to the mast. Editorials are partisan, outspoken, and in case you've missed the point, you can read the articles:

'LABOUR LEFT'S DAY OF HUMILIATION'

'WELFARE SCROUNGERS IN £1 MILLION SWINDLE'

or:

'HEARTLESS MAGGIE PLUMMETS IN POLLS'

'UNEMPLOYMENT CRISIS OUT OF CONTROL'

3   *Yanks don't have national newspapers.*

America is a 'made for TV' nation. This, too, is an accident of geography. Until the advent of recent technology, nation-wide print distribution in a single day was virtually impossible. And, old habits die hard. Today's San Franciscans would rather read the local *Chronicle* than the *Washington Post*. Miami readers take the *Herald* in preference to the *LA Times*. The relatively new *USA Today* has tried to fill the national newspaper gap, but with limited success. It fails to represent a real 'community of interest', and is more a pot-pourri of interesting stories.

Besides . . . in a country as big as America, there are always problems about ads. Who in Seattle cares if Sears Ft Lauderdale is having a tyre sale? The only possible exceptions to this rule, with real claims to National Newspaper-hood are:

1   the *Wall Street Journal*
— Bible to America's share-and-bond-buying, tax-sheltering Super Establishment all over the country, and

2   the *New York Times*
— because everyone everywhere is happy to read ads for Bloomingdale's.

Snigger Press

The 'popular press' in each country adopts a different 'tone of voice'. British tabloids may be explicit, but they are also utterly childish and puerile, figuratively giggling like schoolgirls at the merest mention of anything smutty:

'WHADDA COP-OUT ... SHAME OF THE RED-CHEEKED BOBBY IN THE BUBBLE-BATH'

'PRINCE CHARLES PLAYS WITH HIS WILLIE IN THE POOL'

Brit-press also postures a great deal, and affects a moral view ... which allows canny editors to keep developing a cracking good story, while pretending to play it down:

'PRINCESS MICHAEL'S SECRET ROMANCE ... WHY THE PRESS SHOULD LEAVE HER ALONE'

Ameri-tabloids are less coy, and adopt a straightforward approach. They simply *accuse* people of being drunk, disorderly, romantically linked or morally out-of-bounds. 'Evidence' is not a huge problem; they elevate rumour and gossip to the status of fact, fly a few kites, and are seldom caught out. Yanks can afford to 'publish and be damned'. This is because US libel laws are far less restrictive than Britain's, and editors know that — unless they run afoul of Carol Burnett — they're home and dry.

Which also gives them the right to be unpleasant. If the Brit-press is prurient, Ameri-rag runs often to the downright nauseating:

'3-YEAR-OLD MIRACLE MOM GIVES BIRTH'

'DWARF REMOVES OWN GALL-BLADDER WITHOUT ANAESTHETIC'

'RELIGIOUS FRENZY OF UFO WOMAN'

But, this is splitting hairs. If there are small differences in style between British and American popular papers, there is one major and over-riding similarity. They are all owned by Australians.

The international co-production deal:
Brit-mogul meets Yank-mogul

Today's television industry is a vast sprawl. Deals of mind-bending complexity are daily struck on both sides of the water, to allow executives to off-set the huge risks and costs of production. Known as 'co-production deals' — or sometimes simply as 'pre-sales' — they mean that, after years of splendid isolation, Brit and Yank moguls have finally been forced to do business together.

148

This has come as a shock to both sides. For years, they have professed familiarity with, and respect for, each others' product. In truth, they regard their own as vastly superior, and can't wait to get home and say so to the trade press. Brits think that Yanks are Philistines who pursue ratings at the expense of art; Yanks think Brits lack commercial sense, and tend to deliver 'quirky' programmes short on universal appeal. Often, the relationship ends in tears. But, for Brits heading Stateside (usually the traffic is in that direction) in pursuit of funds, here are a few pointers.

The 11 commandments of international co-production

1 *British and Ameri-TV are simply paced differently,*
   with *news* as the prime example. American news is cut faster and more brutally than Brit-news, and is arguably more demanding to watch. No one spends valuable editing-time looking for smooth and perfectly-matched cut-aways. They knock it out, no frills ... complete with wall-to-wall commentary to cover the joins. The principle extends to documentaries, where the objective is to cut short, keep moving, and sustain excitement.

2 *The pace of non-news programmes (drama, soap, comedy, action-adventure) is different, too*
   Yank-product is action-intensive, with nary a wasted frame. There are no moody, artistic beginnings drawing you slowly into a story. Programme-makers have less than 3 minutes in which to galvanize viewers' attention; and if they can devise an opening sequence which contains a homicide, a sex-attack, a break-dancing sequence, or all three — they will.

3 *Tight dialogue*
   If Yanks talk a lot, characters on TV or in films usually don't. (Rambo had a vocabulary of only 25 words.) With rare exceptions, they rely heavily on action, and do not spend much time throwing *ideas* around ... (though they may express *emotions* openly — 'I only did it because I love ya, buddy' — in a way which does not sit well with Brit-viewers). For the most part, exchanges are kept cryptic and short. If the genre is sit-com, then every line's a laugh-line, or why bother to say it? American sit-coms must be relentlessly

149

'cute' (see 'Cute', Chapter 9), and this, above all, drives Brits mad. They want to build the laugh, preferably by building character — which takes more time. They resist what they see as 'gag writing' . . . and Yanks run out of patience waiting for the jokes.

4 *Eliminate 'grey' areas*

Brits like grey areas, in both character and relationships. (It has something to do with their weather.) They are not fussed if events are inconclusive, or things left hanging, since: (a) life is like that, and (b) such scenarios are intellectually more rigorous. Yanks hate uncertainty, and like matters to be clearly defined. We should know *for sure* if Cagney and Lacey or Starsky and Hutch are gay. Underneath it all, does Archie Bunker really love Edith, or not? Joking aside, what are Hawkeye's real feelings for BJ? Would they die for each other? How about Michael Knight and Kit . . . an emotional attachment, or purely a mechanical one? We should be told. To make things crystal-clear, Yank-writers create opportunities for characters to demonstrate their unspoken devotion, by putting one or the other in mortal danger. Every week.

(Brit-buddies — from *The Likely Lads* to *Minder* — tend to rub along in a more relaxed fashion.)

5 *No equivocal endings*

Brits also like inconclusive *endings*. (That's why they play cricket.) Yanks like things to wrap up nicely. When something ends, it should be *resolved*. Otherwise, TV is too much like life . . . and where's the satisfaction in that? No: Americans see it as TV's job to tie up loose ends. No point in leaving the audience feeling unsettled and restless — unless you're doing a cliff-hanger, and Part 2 is on next week.

6 *Dash of sentiment added*

Yanks are not much drawn to characters who are irredeemably misanthropic . . . even in comedy. They could not love, for example, the Wilfred Bramble character in *Steptoe and Son*. Evil old JR must be seen to shed a tear for the expiring Bobby; selfish Alexis has a soft-spot when it comes to her viperish children. It would be hard to sell Basil Fawlty (or similar) to the major American networks unless the world's least cuddly hotelier was seen to sneak away and give presents to orphans in his spare time.

150

7 *Dispensable authenticity*

US TV moguls are united in the belief that the American public is entirely ignorant of history (i.e., anything that happened prior to the Second World War). Even if viewers have some dim idea of chronology and/or period authenticity, they do not want to take it 'neat', and prefer the 'Walt Disney' version ... as seen in *Rich Man, Poor Man, Winds of War*, and *Jenny's War*.

8 *Star casting*

If Yank moguls are sinking money into an 'historical' blockbuster (see above), they will protect their investment with star casting. Viewers are regularly asked to suspend disbelief and accept, say, Dyan Cannon as Eleanor Roosevelt, Cheryl Ladd as Florence Nightingale, or Catherine Oxenburgh as Eva Peron. This is felt to ensure ratings; furthermore, 'unfamiliar' subjects require the sharp focus a star gives. Brits balk at star casting, and consider it the biggest barrier to international co-production. Stars hijack a production, undermine credibility, and cause dramatic distortions. (Anyway — UK viewers hate seeing American actors in Super-Brit roles.) Many a deal has gone to the wall when Yanks have insisted that, in return for finance, Jane Fonda should play Anne Boleyn/Lady Jane Grey, or want Meryl Streep as the Duchess of Windsor. Sometimes, a compromise is reached, and both sides settle for an unknown with no previous track-record, who also happens to be a second cousin to the Queen.

9 *Moguls in both countries are entirely lacking in confidence*

They do not have the courage of their convictions. They fear constantly for their jobs, and do not wish to be associated with artistic or commercial failure. They therefore hedge their bets by saying 'yes' quite a bit, when what they really mean is 'probably no, but maybe'. Before making final decisions, they test opinion amongst peers, desperately seeking endorsement for their own instinctive views. If they don't get it, they'll change their own instinctive views. Remember that *no one* in television makes decisions alone, but refers them up (or, at top level, *down*). The air whistles with the sound of bucks passing. Too often, Mogul-In-Chief is a capricious Baby-Man, insecure as all the rest. When in doubt, he is likely to be swayed at the eleventh hour by his shrink, his second or third wife, or the last person he spoke to in the elevator.

10 *Never pitch an idea to a Vice-President*

With rare exceptions, he/she has no real power, and will explain your idea badly to someone who has. (Or steal it, leaving you out.) People who have power in Ameri-TV are called: Presidents, Heads of, Controllers of, Executive Editors or Editors-In-Chief. They are seldom female, though Vice-Presidents increasingly are. In fact, every American TV executive *of any stature* is called a Vice-President. It is the next step up from janitor.

11 *Anticipate the game*

Moguls in both countries long ago lost the ability to concentrate. Minds have been blown by trying to process too many electronic data-sources at once. They are now as skittish as viewers, distracted and erratic. Yank-exec is most flamboyant in his looniness. He will:

(a) keep you waiting in an outer office for at least 45 minutes to prove how busy and butch he is. You will wait for a period of time inversely proportionate to his relative importance and security within the organization. A schlep on his way out will make you drum your heels for at least two hours.

(b) wear a baseball cap backwards on his head for the duration of your meeting. Every so often, a colleague will stick his head through the door and yell, 'here, Don — catch!' At this point, Don will playfully snatch a football or baseball from the air, and lose the thread of his conversation with you. Moguls love distractions, which disguise their impaired ability to think. Furthermore, if *you* are sufficiently off-balance, you will not be able to remember the gist of your discussions when it comes to the lawsuit.

(c) continue to take telephone calls all during your meeting, interrupting your pitch 3 or 4 times for long periods. If no one calls *him*, he will call out to see how his second wife, or 14-year-old daughter by a first marriage, got on with her psychiatrist. By the end of the meeting, you will want to grab him by the ears and shake him in order to make him listen. It will do no good. His damaged circuits are on permanent overload. Once you part company and leave, he will forget your name and never return your 'phone calls. This is not a personal slight, since moguls are genetically incapable of returning 'phone calls. (Anyway — if

152

he never speaks to you again, he's freer to pinch your ideas.)
When you finally manage to get through to the office, his
secretary will tell you that 'Don' has been replaced, and
transferred to Atlanta.

24 Police vs. Perps

The Language

YANK-SPEAK =
Cops, Fuzz, Pigs
vs.
Suspects, Crooks, Perps
(perpetrators) or, in New York
City, 'Poips'

BRIT-SPEAK =
Old Bill, Coppers, Bobbies, PCs,
vs.
Villains, Thugs, Hooligans,
Youths, and Helpers with Police
inquiries

BRIT-THINK: *A sentimental view*

Most Brits (of the non-criminal classes) think that their police are wonderful. Police, after all, are in business to preserve and defend the status quo, which is wonderful. Ordinary British coppers do not carry guns, but only truncheons, which is wonderful. Not surprisingly, more and more British thugs seize the opportunity to bring along their own firearms, which is not so wonderful.

Police are generally perceived as long-suffering and brave servants of the community ... guardians of law and order, who — except for the odd rogue — are motivated less by money than a desire to serve. They are almost never black (a fact deeply resented by those criminals who are); and — since they must be 5′8″ or over — rarely oriental or Asian. In more ways than one, the typical British bobby is whiter than white.

In the public mind, the most heinous crime a villain can commit is an attack on a police officer, engaged in the performance of his duties. Brit-thugs are (like all Brits) expected to *play fair*; to observe a code of conduct because it is widely known that the police are unarmed. Increasingly, professional thugs demonstrate their unwillingness to be party to this social contract by trying hard to waste a copper. If caught, they're hit with the full weight of Brit-law. For some reason, taking advantage of a gun-less but fully-trained truncheon-wielding six-footer is considered by the courts to be more reprehensible than attacking defenceless citizens, and often attracts stiffer penalties.

YANK-THINK: It is amazing that any sane person is prepared to join the police, so (glamour-boys in *Miami Vice* notwithstanding) you have to be grateful for what you can get. On that salary, you can't expect genius; just a guy with a hero-complex and an overdeveloped sense of right and wrong. Naturally, they over-react occasionally to stressful situations by gunning down black geriatrics while carrying out eviction orders, or investigating a 'domestic distoibance'. You gotta expect that, and accept that every so often, in the performance of their duties, they'll blow up an entire square block of Philadelphia.

Police have to have guns, or you're asking them to volunteer for suicide. This is the Bronx, not Islamic Jehad. Anyway — they only join the force so they can shoot things. They *like* guns ... remember that it takes a thief to catch a thief. Better to harness their homicidal instincts, and let them work for our side. Lots of them could swing either way.

Of course there's police corruption ... and plenty of it. Whadda ya expect for $20,000 a year — Mother Teresa with a hand-gun? If you want to be truthful, turning a blind eye to rake-offs is the cheapest way for taxpayers to subsidize police salaries. For the most part, they're only stealing from other crooks.

Every so often, a dedicated police officer gets shot in the line of duty, which is a real shame, but after all, he's a big boy. He walks in with his eyes wide open, and he knows what the game is. If you can't stand the heat, you should stay out of the kitchen ... or go run a play-group. He's *paid* to stand in the firing-line and take the first flak from perps to make the streets safe for the rest of us. No one's holding a gun in his back.

25 War games

**AMERI-THINK:** In spite of the fact that the US is arguably the most powerful nation in the world, Yanks are not a warlike people. America was founded by pacifist religious groups who had broken ties with Europe, and the legacy remains. Throughout their short history Americans have formulated or signed many policy documents meant to reduce the possibility of conflict: i.e., the League of Nations Charter, the Monroe Doctrine, the present UN Charter, and the Marshall Plan. They have entered both World Wars late, and with considerable reluctance. In the Sixties, America made Peace and Love fashionable; and by the early Seventies, aversion to war was so widespread that Nixon was forced to extricate America from Vietnam. Yes, average Americans hate fighting ... yet, they are perceived by others as a trigger-happy and Hawkish nation. This is because:

1   they are the world's foremost nuclear power (Might makes Fright)
2   they once 'nuked' Japan
3   they're moving further to the political right, in pursuit of
4   a hard-line Republican president who is not crazy about Communists but loves cowboy novels
5   the successful development of 'Star Wars' could shift the balance of power and leave the US holding the nuclear trump card
6   Yanks may not like fighting foreign wars, but they carry guns and spend a lot of time shooting each other
7   they fight wars in third-world countries by proxy, using CIA operatives with slush funds instead of military troops
8   in matters of foreign policy, they have been known to support right-wing regimes who seem to prefer genocide to Communism
9   they are fully committed to the American Way of Life, and have scant time or tolerance for alternative points of view; and, more important
10   they have 45,000 nuclear warheads, and will not put hands-on-hearts and promise not to use them.

BRIT-THINK: Brits see themselves as a well-behaved people, peace-loving and slow to anger. In fact, they have seldom said no to a good war. They entered with great spirit into the Battle of the Armada, the 100 Years' War, wars about Roses (they have ever been keen gardeners) and any number of colonial wars. They were quick off the mark in the First and Second World Wars, and more recently dispatched a task-force to the Falklands at the first sign of Argie provocation. Mrs T. proclaimed herself 'miffed' at America for invading Grenada, but was happy to send 10 times as many troops 10 times as far from home, to defend one-tenth the number of civilians, and around 10 times as many sheep.

Britain has recently entered a period of heightened anti-American feeling, triggered by the deployment of US cruise missiles in Europe. This mood of antagonism is thought to owe much to successful lobbying by the British Peace Movement for unilateral disarmament. The analysis is not entirely correct. It's true that large numbers of Brits (especially young and politically liberal ones) object to an American military presence in the UK. As an extension of that, more general resentment and mistrust of all things American is commonplace. But it does not follow that average Brits reject nuclear warfare, embrace peace or hate bombs. Evidence suggests that they would simply prefer *British* bombs.

Many Brits now realize that they would have done well to follow De Gaulle's example. His nuclear strategy was essentially 'France for the French'. He insisted upon domestically-made bombs ('French fission'), an independent deterrent, and independent defence. Today, les Frogs are reliable NATO partners and 'contents comme tout' (happy as sandboys), while Brits feel hijacked by the Americans, agonize endlessly about 'dual key', and worry about ending up as a medium-range atomic sacrifice in the clash of the Titans.

26 Religious persuasions

Born (again) in the USA

AMERI-THINK: America was founded by religious dissenters seeking freedom of worship, and is still a bolt-hole for virtually any group, subscribing to any set of beliefs ... however loony. If you wish to find Karma by worshiping sunflowers in the nude while chewing betel nuts and giving all your money to an El Dorado-driving oriental, California has a place for you. This implies that America is a diverse and religiously tolerant nation, which is not strictly true, since in certain parts of the south they beat you up if you don't believe in Jesus.

Presidential candidates from all political parties must show themselves to be both God-fearing and church-going, so as not to alienate the Moral Majority, the Silent Majority, or even plain ol' Middle America. Urban-based, Yuppie-supported liberal Democrats are stuck with the greatest dilemma, since the demands of a national campaign will force them to abandon principles and renounce 'abortion on demand' if they want to get elected ... witness Geraldine Ferraro's desperate compromise: 'I wouldn't choose it for myself, but I believe that all women should have the option.' Nice try. Look where it got her.

Amazing footwork is required in order to curry favour with all disparate religious groups while antagonizing none. Victory to the greatest dancer. Hopefuls must eat bagels and lox with the Jewish community in Brooklyn, then fly off for gravaad lax with Lutherans in Minnesota. They must chew the fat with Irish Catholics in Boston, expressing opposition to the British presence in Northern Ireland, while deftly sidestepping promises of support for the IRA. Not to mention the ERA. God knows, it is not easy.

However: all religious groups in the United States have one thing in common: devotion to fund-raising. In the same way that patriotism merges with show-biz, Amer-religion is tied up with cash; and it is no news to anyone that God is Big Business. The South is awash with video ministers ... influential Fundamentalists who buy TV air-time in order to evangelize on an epic scale. It's a sort of sat-feed of the faithful. And the faithful respond by donating (tax-deductable) millions. Such is the level of American giving, that Yanks have discovered a crossover point between charity and world-domination. Did funds contributed in the United States to NORAID buy the IRA bomb which very nearly wiped out Mrs Thatcher and her Cabinet at Brighton? Did American Sikhs, presently underwriting the rebuilding of the Golden Temple at Amritsar, also engineer the assassination of Mrs Gandhi? And, to what extent is conflict in the Middle East sustained by interest groups Stateside? Who needs the State Department when you can make your own policy at fund-raising dinners, over the chicken-and-lobster in a patty-shell.

BRIT-THINK: Britain is probably the most irreligious nation on earth, which many feel is its great attraction. It is possible to live in some parts of England for years, and never meet anyone who regularly attends a place of

He's got religion, poor chap. Caught it from his girlfriend, apparently.

worship. Most Brits will say, if pressed, that they are 'C of E' ... but reserve the right to do nothing about it. Lack of high-profile — and highly commercialized — religious fervour is one of the more remarkable things about the nation, and may explain much of its political stability.

As ever, Brits mistrust the emotionally-charged, the irrational. They have before them the chastening example of Ireland/Ulster. That way lies madness — which, in any case, is endemic in devout, sectarian countries where people are constantly bashing each other up in the name of God. Look at Spain, France and Italy. The Middle East doesn't bear thinking about. And in the Republic of Ireland and Ulster — the only parts of the UK where religion is a burning issue — there's an orgy of blood-letting, with loony pitted against loony.

No: so far as most Brits are concerned, religious affiliation is a private matter ... slightly embarrassing, like name-of-home-town-and-father's-occupation. It's about obligingly putting on hats to go to weddings, christenings and funerals. Period. Religion should not be allowed to change your way of life, much less deplete your bank account. A few coins in the plate are fine when the church roof has dry rot, but splashy contributions are not called for. Brit-religion has no grandiose, international vision. That's Bob Geldof's job. Anyway — charitable donations are not tax-deductable.

27 Good sport

AMERI-SPORT: It's not 'how you play the game', no siree, sir. It's whether you win or lose. Even more important, it's how you *pay* the game. Professional sportsmen and women have careers which are nasty, brutish and short, so they've a right to pocket what they can while they're young and hot.

Sport in America is three things:

1 another branch of show-biz
2 a ritualized exercise in patriotism and regional loyalty — (i.e., a way of saying 'my country is better than your country', and 'Cleveland is better than Cincinnati')
3 a branch of the *Bank of America* — (i.e., a commercial bonanza for athletes, sponsors and promoters).

Fair play

BRIT-THINK: Brits are respected the world over for the quality of their sportsmanship, and sense of fair play. They are also known for their fondness for amateurism, reluctance to invest in sport, and lack of organized, up-to-date training facilities. This means that Brit-athletes are somewhat hampered, and tend to compete with one set of pectorals tied behind their backs. Internationally, at least, they seldom win anything . . . which they put down to a superior sense of fair play. (Fair play does not extend to Brit fans' treatment of the other team's supporters, which is more like foul play.)

Brits have great patience in sport. That's why they invented cricket, which is an exercise of such subtlety, that only life-long devotees can tell when the ball is actually in play. The moment of maximum spectator appeal comes when players break for tea. Otherwise, games can continue for two or three days with no clear result. Ditto snooker, which lacks the excitement of jai alai, downhill racing or roller-derby, but keeps Brit-audiences glued to tellies in huge numbers for days at a time.

Both Britain and America have 'national' sports (cricket and baseball) which are played in the summer, and get smaller gates than various versions of football (played in the winter) which attract bumper crowds.

162

American football is:

1. a contact sport for those who also enjoy watching head-on collisions between Refrigerators,
2. at college level, a means of awarding athletic scholarships to fellows who count best if it's in yard-lines, and
3. at professional level, an excuse for patriotic displays at half-time, post-game parties, and mega-salaries for anyone who looks like Joe Namath.

Brit-footie is:

1. a means of social mobility, whereby working-class lads — with no other options save jobs down the pits or in rock-bands — can earn a decent living while preserving lungs and eardrums, and
2. a way of letting off steam in public, allowing Brit-fans to pummel each other to a pulp in the stands while players hug and kiss on the pitch.

28 Humour travels?

Transatlantic laughs:

When two countries share a common language it is easy to assume that they also share the attitudes and points-of-reference which are the basic stuff of humour. Yanks and Brits really don't. If proof is needed, remember initial Ameri-bafflement at things Pythonesque. Or how edited highlights of the vastly popular Johnny Carson Show laid a UK egg.

There are, of course, successes as well, which explains the frequent cross-fertilization of TV programmes; but choices must be made with care. Some things won't travel. A Brit trying his favourite Rik Mayall impression on a Yank should prepare for a blank stare. And American

comedienne Joan Rivers leaves her favourite 'K-Mart' jokes out of all her UK routines. The point is that, when your plane leaves LHR or JFK, you leave behind a whole series of cultural references, too.

AMERI-LAUGHS: American humour is about stand-up comics, rooted in Vaudeville and aspiring to Vegas (or a spot on the Johnny Carson Show) with a series of quick-fire gags and one-liners. 'New wave' comics are those who start out at the *Comedy Store* or similar, before moving to Vegas and the Carson Show by way of *Saturday Night Live*.

But, the influence of the 'Greats' — George Burns, Jack Benny — remains. The best (and most exportable) American sit-coms are a collection of high-quality laugh-lines bedded in the matrix of a story: (*M.A.S.H., Rhoda, Cheers*). The most popular funny films feature the likes of Eddie Murphy or Woody Allen, firing gags just as appropriate to the midnight show at Caesar's Palace: 'That's my ex-wife ... I almost didn't recognize her without her wrists cut.' Or: 'Hollywood's so clean! No garbage in the streets — because they put it all on television.' Or: 'Been to Beverly Hills? They're so rich, they watch *Dynasty* to see how *poor* people live. They're so rich, the 7–11 has a fur department.' Or (in *Annie Hall*): 'Nice parking. I can walk to the curb from here.'

To be funny in America, you have to be:

1 a member of an ethnic minority. There are no such things as 'W.A.S.P.' jokes — unless a Jewish comedian tells them.

2 from a large urban area, and (preferably) a deprived background. The scepticism which is the leitmotiv of Ameri-comedy is honed in adversity, which is the same as Brooklyn.

3 a natural cynic, with a tendency toward paranoia. (If you've suffered at the hands of the American medical profession, so much the better.) Life's a mess, human motivation is base, and they're all out to get you anyway. Classic Ameri-comic sees himself as the long-suffering, hard-pressed realist (Jackie Mason, Lennie Bruce, Mort Saul, Bob Hope) ... the last bastion of sanity in a flakey world, knowing the score, telling it 'like it is', keeping his head when, all around him, schnooks are losing theirs. 'I met a guy the other day ... wife's left him, he's got no money and no job. But he's *happy*. Know why? Stupid.'

BRIT-LAUGHS: Modern British humour also derives from Music Hall — which is the rough equivalent of Vaudeville. It, too, is urban in outlook ... though only *specific* urban areas will do. People from northern cities like Manchester and Liverpool are funny, because the alternative is suicidal despair. (In some northern towns, suicide is redundant.) Rural areas do not generate humour (Brits take the countryside too seriously) and Chipping Sodbury has produced few great comics.

Londoners can be funny, but only if they're from the East End — with the chirpy, street-smart, wide-boy sense of humour which that implies. You can poke fun *at* people who come from NW3, or Islington or Surbiton. No one funny has ever come from Twickenham, Croydon, or Friern Barnet ... though comedians from the East End who have made money hurry to live there.

To be funny in Britain, you have to:

1 portray yourself as a loser and nitwit. It is *you* who are out of step with the rest of society, *you* who march to the beat of a different drummer. Brit-comic often plays the nerd, or the loony. Classic example is John Cleese as Basil Fawlty; or Morecambe and Wise, vying with each other to see who is the bigger nincompoop. Ditto the Two Ronnies, or Pete and Dud ... the unselfconsciously hopeless, pitted against a world which is basically sane. Then came Python, in which the world *and* the people in it were mad, and followed to the letter the logic of their own lunacy: summarize Proust competitions and parrot sketches, and

'Buried the cat last week.'
'Was it dead?'
'No, we just didn't like it very much.'

2 be brave about death. (Yank-comics won't touch it with a barge-pole ... and Ameri-audiences don't believe in it anyway.) But north of Watford, the sense of humour is sub-fusc black. Nothing raises a bigger laugh than a good death or funeral joke:

DOCTOR (TO PATIENT): ... You're in great shape. You'll
live to be 90.
PATIENT: ... I *am* 90.
DOCTOR: ... Oh, well. That's it, then.

Even Python raised its biggest laugh with a sketch about an ex-parrot who had gone to meet its Maker and was nailed to its perch.

166

3   neutralize female sexuality. Women are not the air-headed, full-
    bosomed sex-objects of Ameri-comedy, but more often the beefy
    and relentless predators who come between men and their
    preferred pursuits. Red-blooded northern males would rather be
    down 'at t'pub', or playing darts with 't'lads', while leaving the
    little woman to exhaust her libido by mending the roof on the
    garden shed. The north is a Man's World. And when death
    finally comes to claim the menfolk, northern women can scarcely
    tell the difference.

There's one more quirk about Anglo-American humour. It has to do
with *which* ethnic or regional groups are perceived as figures of fun.
Yanks tell Polish jokes, while Brits — who never knew that Poles were
specially hopeless — enjoy Irish jokes. They'll also send up Aussies:
('mind if I call you Bruce, Bruce?') or people from Neasden ('Neasditz'),
but haven't hooked into the whole idiom of 'Californian' jokes.
EXAMPLE:

QUESTION:	How many Californians does it take to change a light-bulb?
ANSWER:	12. One to screw it in, and 11 to share the experience.
	OR:
QUESTION:	What's 'Californian' for 'boy, am I ever gonna screw you up.'
ANSWER:	'Trust me, trust me.'*

*(seekers after co-production deals, p.148, please take note)

29 Glamour-US

Glamour U.S.

Yanks adore it, live for it. Glamour is external evidence of 'Having It All' — the Ameri-dream and aspirational apotheosis. 'If I've one life to live,' said the TV commercial, 'let me live it as a blonde.' Preferably Krystal Carrington. After all, it's claimed that we pass this way but once . . . and a high-glam life is some compensation for death, in case it turns out to be compulsory.

Americans understand that glam is power: POWER-GLAM. It impresses others, who believe that 'what you see is what you get'. Proper packaging can seduce the world, and — in the process — transform the schlep beneath: approval = confidence, confidence = success. Glam can percolate down and change a person's soul. It's admired by Yanks in the way that Brits admire breeding, arousing desire and respect. It turns the ordinary into the extraordinary, and the merely passable into more perfect people. POWER GLAM works from the outside *out*, and the outside *in* . . . which is what the Fairy Godmother did for Cinderella.

Blinded by the light and utterly star-struck, Americans will buy anything which they associate with glamour, in case it rubs off. They snap up bedsheets designed by Halston or Calvin Klein, as slept on by Liza Minelli or Cher. They stock up on 'personality' perfumes — 'testimonial fragrances' endorsed by Joan Collins ('Scoundrel'), Linda Evans ('Forever Krystal'), or Sophia Loren ('Sophia'). Oh, the thrill of sharing Super-Glam for only a small investment. Some call it the Ameri-triumph of form over substance; but for the average Ms America with expendable cash, 'Having It All' — the high-quality life — means looking good. Looking good means looking like the stars. Also sleeping on their sheets, and smelling like them if possible.

BRIT-THINK: Testimonial fragrances never caught on in Britain. Gallons of Sophia, Krystal and Joan languish forlornly on UK cosmetic counters. They have no natural market, since:

1 young Brit-ettes are turned on by *glam-rock* (i.e., Madonna), not haute-bourgeois Hollywood glam, and,
2 middle-aged Brits in most income-groups have no real feeling for glam, and are impervious to the seductions of the High Life, preferring the Home Counties.

Brits (especially those living north of Watford) are wholly unmoved and unimpressed by the razzmatazz of Ameri-glam, and do not comprehend its appeal. It has nothing to do with them. They are content to admire from afar (e.g., Princess Diana), but have no desire to imitate, participate in, or buy a piece of. You will never catch one sleeping on a Selina Scott sheet.

This is, of course, because their aspirations are so different, having less to do with the glitter of Hollywood, than the more subtle incandescence of birthright and glittering prizes. Brits sigh for the pleasures of 'being there', solid and entrenched. 'Getting there' looks suspiciously vulgar. Cornerstones of Brit-life — like Old Money, Family Background, the social order — are resolutely anti-glam, since glam confers power on the unworthy, and carries with it more than a hint of social mobility. The important thing to know about money, glamour, and similar externals, is that they don't change what you *are*. Yanks never understand that.

Victoria Principal? Take away the clothes, the jewellery, the make-up, the hair the beautiful figure, the lovely smile, the money, and what have you got?

30 The final solution: or, What *really* counts

BRIT-THINK: If there's one thing that True Brits have, it's a sense of priorities. When all is said and done, only *two things* really count; and — singly or together — they are the quintessence of Brit-life:

1 **The Royal Family**
... beloved of everyone — even the long-term unemployed and Scargillian socialists, who would gladly smash the system, but leave intact every hair and ostrich feather on the Queen Mum's head. The Royals *are* Britain. They're WHAT WE'RE ABOUT, and DUTY, and HOW WE DO THINGS and WE'VE ALWAYS DONE IT THIS WAY ... a diamond-studded bulwark against any form of social change. Ever.
They are contentment ... human incarnations of qualities and spiritual values which transcend hard cash. Royals inhabit a Higher Plane, since they are so rich that they need never concern themselves about money. Brits draw comfort from that.

2 **The Pub**
... focal point of Brit-life, the Great Leveller (the *only* leveller) which unites dustmen and kings. Pubs are comfortable and comforting — places where average Brits can rehearse cosy thoughts and attitudes, sure of endorsement and a sympathetic hearing from others too smashed to notice.
Brits only make it through a working morning by looking forward to drinking lunch in the nearest pub, then remain groggy for most of the working afternoon, surfacing just in time to grab a 'quick one' at 6 p.m. before starting for home and an evening's telly, followed by a nip down to the local for 'last orders' at 11.00 ... which ensures the residual hang-over which dulls work-performance the next morning until it's time to break for a pub lunch — and so on.
In pubs, Brits put problems to rights, re-assure everyone about everything, blow all surplus cash, and escape the pressures of family

170

life for a glorious hour or two. Pubs are 'public' in the true sense of the word, since women on their own, or gaggles of 'girl-friends', or OAPs are welcome, as long as they all agree to abandon children on the doorstep.

Having attracted said custom, the average neighbourhood pub sets about withdrawing all services — i.e., warm drinks, no selection, no ice, no hot drinks, no acceptable food, nowhere to sit and unspeakable wallpaper. This makes patrons feel right at home; and they get on with the serious business of doing what they do best in pubs. Being British.

Double raspberry ripple to go

AMERI-THINK: Americans, for all their affluence and the distractions it can bring, know what really counts. ICE CREAM. More than allegiance to the flag, or a national newspaper, or to Johnny Carson, or the micro-chip, it's mocha-chip (and peppermint crunch) that binds the nation together. Fail to appreciate this, and you've missed out on the quintessence of Ameri-culture. Ice cream is the Great Leveller . . . the Yank version of pubs. It is the fixed point in an otherwise mobile society, guaranteed to give pleasure to all. Americans will drive 100 miles for the ultimate cone. Don't ask why. Debates about the MX missile are taken no more seriously than where you can find the best coffee flavour in Los Angeles. It's the American way of saying that, at bottom, stripped bare of affectation, they know what life is about — and you can always appeal to them successfully on that level. Understand this, and you've gone a long way to zeroing in on Ameri-think. So, pack your 'I ♥ NY' T-shirt and your LA address book, and prepare for fun. Don't worry about a thing. If you can't get to grips with the Great American Dream, you can fall back on the Great American Cream. Mint chip is nice.

The Special Relationship

Things Yanks will never understand about Brits, and vice versa

YANKS (ON BRITS)

1 Aren't they cold?
2 What's a stone, and how many make a person? Can you wear one in a ring?
3 Who invented the toast-rack? Is there a national preference for hard, cold toast?
4 Have they thought of selling electrical appliances complete with plugs?
5 Why do they make their summer travel arrangements in *January*? How do they know they'll *live* 'til July?
6 What's a diary? Did Anne Frank have one? Why do women like them full, and businessmen like them empty?
7 Do they throw you out of the country if you don't have net curtains?
8 Why do they write to say they'll 'phone, then 'phone, then write to confirm the call?
9 What's the point of 'queuing up' at railway stations in order to get on trains?
10 Why is it called a 'Bank Holiday' when the whole nation wants to travel, and so British Rail closes down?
11 What's the great attraction of baked beans without the hot dogs?
12 Don't they feel the lumps in the mattresses?

BRITS (ON YANKS)

1 Why are all American women 'interior decorators' — except the ones who are real estate brokers?
2 Why do they buy six of everything they like?
3 Why do they see at least three doctors every time they get sick?
4 What is the recreative value of returning merchandise to shops?
5 Can't they think of better ways to spend an evening than driving 30 miles for ice cream?
6 What's the point of calling taxi drivers 'sir'?
7 Why do they plan everything at the last minute, then want it 'now'?
8 What's the secret of the national obsession with Filo-fax?
9 Will anything persuade them to answer letters and return calls?
10 Why do they think bread tastes better if you put a hole in the middle, and call it a bagel?
11 How come staff in American restaurants only tell you to 'have a nice day' when it's time to leave a tip?
12 Why do even little old ladies chew gum?

YANKS (ON BRITS)

13 Are some people tall enough to *step over* the sides of the baths?
14 Will penicillin cure a spotted dick?
15 Why do they spend their working lives trying to get knighthoods, when there's no money in it?
16 Is the 'old boys' network' a lobby-group for the senile?
17 Have they lost the will to live because:
    (a) the weather's foul,
    (b) they have to pack their own groceries at supermarkets, *and* pay for the bags,
    (c) they don't have good ice cream?

BRITS (ON YANKS)

13 Don't they know how they look in shorts?
14 Where do all of them get all the money?
15 Why do total strangers approach you like long-lost friends, ask you for cigarettes, and invite you to dinner? When you show up, why can't they remember your name?
16 Do quite *normal* people enjoy peanut-butter-and-jelly sandwiches?
17 Are there Americans who live and die without ever emerging from a shopping mall?

And try finding an egg-cup anywhere in the U.S.A!